# SPECIAL CHILDREN, SPECIAL GOD

# Special Children, Special God

**UNA MENNISS**

with

**JANE COLLINS**

**KINGSWAY PUBLICATIONS**

**EASTBOURNE**

*Front cover photo: Zefa Picture Library*

**British Library Cataloguing in Publication Data**

Menniss, Una
    Special children, special God.
    1. Handicapped children. Mothers. Biographies
    I. Title    II. Collins, Jane
    362.40852

ISBN 0–86065–794–9

*Certain names have been changed
in the interests of confidentiality*

Printed in Great Britain for
KINGSWAY PUBLICATIONS LTD
1 St Anne's Road, Eastbourne, E Sussex BN21 3UN by
Richard Clay Ltd, Bungay, Suffolk
Typeset by Watermark, Crostwight, Norfolk

# CHAPTER ONE

It seemed like only five minutes before it started again. My whole body tensed at the sound, although I wanted nothing more than to relax. Moving very slowly so as not to disturb Alec, asleep beside me, I peered into the dark at the clock. Three o'clock. A little groan escaped me. So long to survive till the morning! So short a time to sleep!

But sleep didn't appear to be an option. From down the landing came the rhythmic thumping and squeaking which, for the last six months, had haunted my days and destroyed my nights.

The squeak was the protest of Paul's cot as it was rocked back and forth. The thump, thump, thump was his head banging slowly, methodically, against the end of the cot.

Numbly, I tensed myself against the cold and slid out of bed. My dressing-gown and slippers were ready on the chair from the last expedition, but I decided not to bother. It was a sort of promise to myself that it wouldn't take long. I fumbled at his door and sighed at what I knew I would see: our one-year-old son, apparently normal and healthy, on his hands and knees in his cot, intent on hurting himself.

Automatically I pulled him away, back down the cot, straightened the pillow which we put at the end of the bed to get in his way, and tucked him up again. There was no reaction from him: not a flicker of recognition in his eyes. As usual he was distant, remote. This didn't stop me bending down to kiss him and smooth back his fringe. It was an automatic gesture, like all the others in my torpid state, but it was still important. Surely if I showed him love, things could only improve. Sometimes I felt more like strangling him, but the hugs and kisses were a pledge to myself, born of a conviction that inside that emotionless shell was a loving, responsive little boy. That conviction needed bolstering many times every day. For now, however, silence. Back to bed.

Desperate for sleep though I was, I couldn't still the strident voices of my anxiety running over and over the same ground, optimism and pessimism battling it out in my mind.

'It can't be right. There must be something wrong.'

'But that letter on the problem page said it often happened, and it was quite normal.'

'You can't believe that. It's not just the head-banging. What about the way his eyes never meet yours? When did you ever see him smile at you? You know jolly well there's something wrong.'

'But no doctor thinks so. Anyway, I prayed and prayed that he would be normal. Especially since his older brother is so slow.'

'Just because Richard is retarded, it doesn't mean that there can't be anything wrong with Paul.'

'But that's just the point. Richard was very slow at everything: sitting up, crawling. He didn't walk until he was two and a year later he's got very few words. Paul is quite different. He rushes around like a mad thing, very inquisitive – the doctor said he was intelligent.'

6

'But why will he never let you put him on your lap or cuddle him? Why does he sit rocking backwards and forwards for hours?'

'At least he's happy!'

'Until you try to make him do something he doesn't want to!'

'But all children are like that... aren't they?'

On and on, my thoughts dragged me round in circles. I hoped for the best, but really my situation was not good. Richard, at four, was quite severely handicapped mentally, and now his little brother was showing these alarming behaviour patterns. The doctors could give no reason for either of their problems – indeed, when it came to Paul they made me think I was making a fuss about nothing. True, I didn't have a 'normal' son to compare him with, and Richard was so placid that any child would look hyperactive beside him. Yet I couldn't shake off the conviction that Paul was not normal either.

Perhaps it was the rejection of any physical contact, any sign of affection, that really worried me the most. Even in his sleep he flinched away from me. The memory of that was like a new pain, like stubbing your toe when you've got a headache. It was bad enough that he might have some problem – worse if he rejected my help. I knew myself well enough to realise that I was sinking emotionally, and would lie here in misery for hours if I didn't break out of the vicious circle.

Only one thing could ever calm the panic, stem the tidal wave of self-pity. Many times a day, and again now, I turned to God. It was quite an effort to pray rather than to wallow in worry, but I knew no other way to lift the weight off me. Sleepy as I was, I could only think a few Godward phrases.

'Lord, I'm frightened again. Hold me, Lord.'

Sometimes I was sure God got weary of me and my troubles. Yet each time, sometimes quietly, sometimes like the sun bursting through cloud, I would sense that

God was there, loving me. Suddenly a phrase from the Old Testament slipped into my mind. 'Underneath are the everlasting arms.'

Yes, that was it. That was what it felt like. As surely as my mattress supported my exhausted body at the moment, so even in the worst moments God's love was under me, like a sort of mattress, to stop my downward fall into a pit of despair. Just to think that God was there meant that I could relax, however much my fears spun me round and round. He would hold me. I snuggled down into the mattress. My thoughts meandered on, but the edge of fear was taken away.

I can't remember when I first turned to God as a child. From before memories began I had trusted him, and my childhood had taught me that very little in this world is trustworthy. Not that I was badly treated, exactly. But there was never any security.

Mother was a semi-invalid all her life. As a child I knew nothing about septicaemia, only that sometimes Mother was very ill in hospital, and then I couldn't live at home.

Every day I prayed Mummy would get better. Then when I was eleven, a new vaccine was made available, and Mother, although never strong, recovered sufficiently to be able to live a more or less normal life.

This was the answer to my prayer! My faith in God, so often rejected by children at about that age, became firm and vital. Now church no longer bored me, and I prayed quite a lot, in a child-like way. I desperately wanted to be confirmed, but was told I had to wait until I was fifteen, when I would really understand what it was all about. I was most indignant.

At last, I was admitted to confirmation classes. There I was told that the cross showed us that 'I', our selfish ways, had to be crossed out. I was very eager to do this for Christ, because he had healed my mother. Yes, God was good. I had always trusted him in the past, and now, however rough things became, I would go on trusting him.

There. I was beginning to relax in God's love, at last.

But would my toes never warm up? I turned over and moved them carefully closer to Alec: not actually to touch him and make him cold, but just to feel his warmth from a little way off.

I sighed. It suddenly came to me that this was a picture of the spiritual communication between Alec and me these days. I longed to be closer to him, to share my faith with him. After all, it was the most important area of my life. But if I got too close, he would back off. What had gone wrong? When we met, his faith seemed as firm as mine, and he was a much stronger person. He had been wounded in the war and had had an artificial limb fitted, because he had lost a leg in action, but he was a tower of strength – practical and warm-hearted. Most importantly, he shared my Christian faith.

But now, over five years later, it was hard to remember the times when we went to church or read the Bible together. Six months after we married the spiritual aspect of our relationship stopped, suddenly and completely.

'All my life I've gone to church to please other people. There might be a God up there, but I don't know where Christ fits in, and I'm fed up with pretending I do.' This was all the explanation I got.

I prayed hard for Alec, but his reaction was so cold when I tried to talk to him about my faith. After a few attempts at this, I learned to keep Alec and God in two separate compartments because it hurt me so much to hear my husband explicitly rejecting the mainspring of my life. I knew this wasn't ideal, but it was the only way I could survive.

So now, as I lay beside him, I prayed again that even as his warm body had revived mine, so my faith would revive his.

Suddenly I jolted back into wakefulness.

Thump ... thump ... thump ...

I must have slept through several minutes of this, because Alec was stirring. If I didn't move quickly, he would be getting up, but it was such a long job for him because he had to put on his artificial leg.

'It's OK. I'm awake.'

This time I did stop for my slippers. The landing was very cold. It's a wonder Paul doesn't get cold with the blankets off like that. At least he has the airing cupboard in his room. Just a minute, airing cupboard. Pillows. What if ...

Sitting Paul abruptly at the bottom of the cot, I wedged two pillows under the top end of the mattress. Now he had to climb a hill before he could reach the top of the cot. It was worth a try.

Lie him down, tuck him in, a quick kiss whether he wants it or not, and back to bed.

'Lord, give me peace. Peace about Alec, peace about Richard and Paul. Lord, give me love. You have given them to me to love, and I do love them. Help me to love them as they are, even if they aren't what I expected, even if I don't understand them.

'Lord, let me sleep so I can love again tomorrow....'

# CHAPTER TWO

Six months later, nothing much had changed. I was so worn down by coping with one day at a time that I hadn't the energy to wonder how the reality of my life could be so different from my expectations. Richard was happy and loving, but unmistakably retarded, and Paul's behaviour was so erratic and violent that I was continually on my guard. Alec was a tower of strength in practical ways, but wasn't prepared to give God any space.

'Why on earth do you want to get up early on a Sunday for Communion? It's the one day I can be here to let you have a lie-in. You're so tired. What you need is a break!'

I hadn't begun to think about a holiday. It just seemed impossible. Then my Auntie Elsie in Colchester wrote and offered to have us to stay for a week.

Auntie had an optimism that was infectious: surely with an extra pair of hands and new surroundings for Paul to explore he would be manageable. As he had grown and become mobile, his behaviour had become more and more strange. There seemed to be no pattern,

11

except he was always surprising us, and draining us of every ounce of strength. He loved climbing: out of his cot, into the open top drawer, over the garden wall, any obstacle was a challenge. His safety was a constant problem. Still, Aunt was quite right that we all needed a holiday. For weeks Alec had been coming home tired from work to find chaos and me at the end of my tether. A change would do us all good. I pushed my apprehension aside and we set off.

It was indeed a tonic at least to share the pandamonium with another adult all day long: I could concentrate on the boys knowing that a meal would be ready on time, or on another day I could do the dinner without several trips out of the kitchen to check what that noise was – or that silence!

On Sunday, joy of joys, Alec offered to keep an eye on the boys while I went to church with Auntie. A weekly diet of a cold walk alone to 7.30 Morning Communion with at most half a dozen people was keeping me going spiritually, but only just. This morning's service was nothing special to the others there, perhaps, but for me it was like a feast, and I walked home chattering animatedly to Auntie and smiling at anyone who met my eyes.

Which was exactly what Alec couldn't do as he opened the door on our return. He turned back into the hall without a word, but his body communicated a brokenness which immediately diminished my joy.

'What's the matter?' I blurted as I followed him into the house, not bothering to take off my coat.

'You'd better come and see.' His mumble hardly reached me. Silenced, Auntie Elsie and I followed him into the garden. The boys were now playing with the toys we had put out in the middle of the lawn for them, but around them the devastation told us they hadn't been there all morning. All over the little winding paths lay the uprooted plants from the flower borders, trampled down with muddy shoes as Paul had run round and round much too fast for Alec, who was hampered by his artificial leg.

'Poor Alec,' said my magnificent Auntie. 'I'll make you a cup of tea.'

I couldn't follow her example. I bore down on Paul, who didn't seem to have noticed our arrival, and started shouting at him, shaking him by the shoulder. He just looked puzzled, although I knew he understood the words I was using.

'Why not? What are they for, anyway? I just felt like it,' he seemed to imply.

'Poor flowers,' I said sadly to him, but there was no response in his eyes. 'Poor flowers,' I repeated to myself, going over to rescue some of the crushed blooms. The lavenders, crushed by the trampling, gave off a heavy scent, and I found I was blinking back tears. One brief hour of freedom for me, and something, somewhere, had to suffer. I couldn't blame Alec. He looked as crushed as the flowers, bewildered by his failure and the senseless destruction that had gone on. He had tried so often to come to terms with our house always being in such a state, but now I sensed a new depth of understanding of our plight. I went to hold his hand, and we leaned against each other, facing the mess, a symbol of the wreckage of our lives.

'It's all right, love, I know how you feel.' My voice cracked.

'Why?' he whispered, mournfully. 'But why?' He sighed.

Why indeed? There was no answer to the question which I asked myself so many times a day, so in the end I got on with life as it was. Sometimes, Paul's antics were quite amusing, like the next afternoon when Auntie sent Alec and me out for a walk together and afterwards proudly announced that Paul had made, and consumed, his own tea – a mixture of raw egg, butter and marmite!

Paul just didn't add up. He lived in a world of his own,

13

and didn't relate to us at all. He didn't even look at us, let alone smile, but sometimes a giggle would escape him for no reason at all. He could speak clearly, but hardly ever said anything. If nothing was happening, he would rock – back and forward, back and forward. Three kitchen chairs simply fell to pieces after a few weeks of his rocking. He seldom played with toys, but would spend hours crawling around on the stairs, devising odd patterns of movement which seemed to satisfy him in some way. We wondered whether his destructiveness were due to boredom, but when we invited a little girl exactly his age to tea he completely ignored her, and she was very upset. This experiment was a failure, except that it made very clear to me that Paul had a big problem. A local clinic doctor called him 'an extreme individualist'. Eventually we consulted a paediatrician, who listened to us, watched Paul, and offered his opinion that Paul was 'an interesting case'. I could have thrown something at him. I wanted to know what was wrong. How could we contain him? How could we train him in some way? What discipline could we use?

Sometimes, just sometimes, we could win one over on him. He went through periodic bouts of not eating, and would get very thin. During one of these, when all he would eat was pink blancmange, we used cochineal to colour his food pink: pink mashed potato, pink butter, pink soup... and it worked!

Poor Richard stood a good chance of being overlooked in all this. We decided that we should give him as good a start as possible at school, and when he was four stretched ourselves to afford a private kindergarten. This seemed to pay off, as he was in a small class with a motherly teacher whom he adored. He was teased sometimes, because his speech was very jumbled, and he was so affectionate and trusting that the teasing bewildered him, but in general he enjoyed school. He even made a reasonable start on his reading. My worries about him were now

14

quite overshadowed by Paul.

I had always wanted more than two children, and despite the horror of our situation, felt we should have another. Alec was amazed, and anxious. I prayed that if it was God's will, Alec would change his mind without me going on about it. Gradually, Alec came to agree with me, and when I found I was pregnant, he looked forward to the birth of our third child as much as I did. I was convinced I would have a lovely daughter.

Not that it could ever be an easy pregnancy with Paul around. He went off his food, cried for hours on end, and all four of us developed racking coughs which disturbed all our nights and took us weeks to get over in our cold, damp house. There was a boiler in the kitchen, and a coal fire in the living room, but the warmth of these didn't penetrate into the hall, and upstairs was miserable.

At last the spring came, and I watched the crocuses dance for joy... until Paul did another of his uprooting tricks. I smacked him quite hard, but the very next day he went back and finished off the job. Nothing deterred him.

One day he smashed the mixing bowl and got a taste for the sound: a few days later a plate went flying out of the door. One bath time, while I was fetching a towel from the adjoining room, he drank from a bottle of camphorated oil, which meant a dash to the doctor. He terrified me by climbing into the top branches of the apple tree, swaying violently. He scattered coal all over the garden which I was too pregnant to do much about – Alec did it when he came home. He developed a craze for investigating the drains. He frequently broke windows.

All his movements were like lightning, and if this was bad at home, out shopping it was much worse. He had no fear of roads, crowds, or strange places, and never stayed by my side unless I had a good grip on him. One day I saw him making a bee-line towards the door of the shop and out into a busy street, and I fell heavily as I ran after him.

15

Being obviously pregnant, I was offered a lot of help from passers-by, but this embarrassed me. I went home without finishing my shopping. Without a stream of prayers to God to help me I could never have got through this long period, and I am sure that my prayers prevented me from doing physical damage to Paul, as I was often at the end of my tether.

Just before I went into the maternity home, Paul fell from a tree and injured his leg: the doctor sent him to hospital for investigation. I was really worried about the effect this would have on him, and sent with him the only thing he really cared about – his teddy bear, with name and address firmly marked on a tape.

On August 14th our daughter was born, perfect as I had known she would be, and we were filled with joy and given a new hope for the future. We called her Philippa.

Meanwhile Paul came home from hospital to find me replaced by an unknown housekeeper. He had a spiral fracture just above the ankle, held tight with a large crêpe bandage, which didn't seem to stop him getting around. But he had lost his teddy. I came home to a very disturbed Paul.

Richard soon adjusted to having his baby sister around, and obviously loved her, helping me to look after her. Paul couldn't have cared less. I worried that he would attack her in some way, which he could have done out of spite or unintentionally. I prayed about this, and it never happened. Our worries then focused on his food, as he would eat nearly nothing and grew frighteningly thin. As the weather grew colder again he really suffered, and one day I found him shut into the airing cupboard, nearly passing out with the heat. After this, Alec fixed the door partly open so that it could warm his room a little. His eating improved marginally. On his birthday he stuffed himself with cake and was then horribly sick! The turning point in his eating came when at Christmas I gave him a teddy as similar as possible to the one lost in the hospital.

He took to it immediately, and the eating problems were over.

Now that baby Pips was in the house, my days were full, but not in the happy way I had expected from a young family. There was crisis after crisis with Paul, anger and frustration and fear ricocheting in my head all day long and draining me even more than the physical effort of running after him and tussling with him. I tried to get out, but this just increased the danger factor. Paul had no road sense and could dash across a road without warning, or run out to pick something up.

Alec was a meticulous keeper of diaries, working over the little books in tiny writing during his lunch breaks at work. Later he copied them into school notebooks which I didn't read for many years, but which add another perspective to my own memories. For example at this time he frequently recorded that 'Una is very tired and wakes up with headaches' or 'Una had a bout of nerves and got very upset, so helped her to bed early' or 'Una on edge and awake most of the night'.

What a welcome break it was at the weekends when Alec could take us out in the car to the country. I didn't have to worry about traffic, and the open sky allowed my spirit to breathe again. My passion for flowers could be indulged as I wandered along, and without these breaks I could never have got through the weeks. Alec's salary was quite limited, and we could only afford a car because of his disability pension, but we considered it a necessity. His work as a lithographic artist required great concentration, and at the weekend we both needed to relax.

Some of God's care was expressed to me through my beloved Alec. Day after day he would arrive home from work to a chaotic house, but after tea he would set about washing up, bringing in the coal, tackling most of the washing and ironing, and some of the mending.

Now and then, understandably, it would all get too much for him, and he would snap, 'I'm fed up with this chaos. Surely you can do better than this. You ought to be able to find some way of controlling Paul.' I would fly into a violent temper, justifying myself, and we would then spend several hours simmering down in a painful silence. Gradually, the anger would evaporate, until by the end of the day we could see each other's point of view. Our love for each other was too deep for rows to last long.

My annual great escape was a 'Family Holiday Week' organised by the Mothers' Union at a boarding school near Exmouth. Our first visit was so successful that we went again the next year. There were volunteer helpers with the children, and the perfect mixture of games and outings to the beach for the children, with discussions and worship and friendships to be made among the adults. After this experience I began taking the boys to church sometimes, even if their good behaviour there was compensated by some dreadful deed when they got home. Alec, too, went to Communion for a while after this holiday. He never came with me, though, and never talked about it.

'I wish we could go together some time,' I ventured wistfully one damp Sunday.

'Oh, there's no point really,' he said dismissively. 'What I do in church is private, between me and God. It's not something I could share.' My face fell, but he was already on his way upstairs, and didn't notice.

At this time Richard was nearing seven, and would soon have to leave his school. He had no concept of number beyond counting to three, but his reading was quite impressive. Our hope was that we would be given some financial help to send him to a special school for older children. Nevertheless a visit with both boys to the County Psychologist resulted in the statement that both boys were retarded.

This apparently didn't mean they would have special schooling. Quite the reverse. This was before the 1970 Education Act, and you could quite simply be refused any

18

education at all if your child was deemed 'ineducable'.

Alec's diary records that he was 'annoyed, frustrated and indignant', and even that hardly did justice to what I felt, faced with endless days of all three children at home. Eventually, the County agreed that both boys could have a trial at the local primary school. This was second best, as we felt they needed special schools with more individual teaching. Still, however doubtful we were of the wisdom of this plan, we had no choice but to try it.

To compound the problem, we seemed to spend all winter struggling against colds, coughs, tummy bugs, mumps, just one thing after another. Perhaps it was because my energy was already so stretched that this seemed like the last straw. I was trapped at home, never overcoming the chaos, and frightened when I went out. Paul became more and more difficult on walks. Every few yards he would take a few steps backwards, or stop to examine the soles of his shoes. You couldn't jolly him out of it, or threaten him. It was a fixation, and the only thing that mattered to him. It seemed to threaten his very identity if you challenged him, so you just had to be patient.

On other occasions he would be what I called 'fixed': he would just stop, wherever he was, and would not be moved. Once he did this in the middle of the road, and I had no choice but to drag him to the pavement and sit him down on a low wall, where he sobbed and sobbed as if his heart would break. I wanted to hold him, but he fought me off, and I had to rub at the stinging of my own unshed tears as we straggled home, defeated... again.

# CHAPTER THREE

Amazingly, when Paul started school, he seemed quite containable. I certainly felt as though I prayed him through every minute. He didn't relate to the other children, but seemed to enjoy himself. One day he threw his teddy onto the roof of a single storey classroom, and while the teacher struggled with a window pole, Paul went to the rescue up the drainpipe, encouraged by a roar of admiration from the other children. For several months I began to have hope, and there are several anecdotes from that time which any mother might have, such as the snowman. Although I had to do most of the work of building it, it was a great success until it started to thaw and the head rolled off. Paul was so distressed that he brought it into the house to look after it!

One of the greatest problems I faced was loneliness. Other mothers take their children out, go to play with other children, or at least get out in the evenings from time to time. Any of these escapes seemed impossible.

'Lord, send me a friend,' I pleaded, and then added, as

if afraid to ask for too much, 'and can it be someone who loves you too?'

A boy in Paul's class lived quite near, and we would often see him and his mother making their way along the same road as us. Gradually we started waiting for each other so we could talk our way to school. This had been going on for some time, and it didn't occur to me that God would actually be providing the answer to my prayer before I prayed it.

Then one day the mother, Audrey, said, 'You know, I pray for you and your boys every day.' With this assurance I knew that Audrey was the answer I should have been looking for, and so began a friendship which was to sustain me through many years to come.

One effect of school was that as Paul's speech caught up with his limited desire to communicate, he stopped doing the very detailed drawings which had surprised us at first, but which we later understood to be in place of speech. After a Mr White had done some plumbing in the house, Paul had done a picture of a house full of pipes, taps and a bath. He drew a knocker on the door, knocked a few times, then said, 'Mr White not at home.' Then he laughed, shaded in the bathroom window and explained, 'Mr White having bath!'

Unexpectedly, to me at least, I went through a long period when I felt I just couldn't pray. I was tired of telling God what I wanted, and although I often received the strength I asked for, in the long term nothing was changing. There seemed little point in praying. I wanted some sort of understanding of my situation from God's point of view. Eventually, I was reduced to the phrase, 'Oh God, speak to me.' For several days I pleaded with God, and suddenly in my mind came the words 'divine healing' and the conviction that I had to go and talk to my vicar about it.

Now Canon Lambert was a compassionate man, and a good listener, but he had never to my knowledge mentioned God's power to heal, and I felt so nervous of broaching the subject with him that I stopped in at the church on the way to pray for courage. I needn't have worried: he was wonderful.

'This is a message from God,' he said seriously, 'and we must act on it. I don't know very much about this sort of thing, but give me a fortnight to find out more, and then we'll talk again.' In that time he contacted a friend, the Revd Harding, who had an active healing ministry, and arranged for a service of anointing for Paul and Richard on the Sunday after Easter. Now it was Alec's reaction I trembled about, because he very rarely went to church, and never with me. Against my expectations he said he would come, and chatted it over with the vicar. My hopes soared.

Eight days before the service, I was making a bed when suddenly I was aware of another personality in the room with me. Christ himself was there, looking at me with compassion. I dropped to my knees. I couldn't actually see him, but his presence was so real I felt that if he moved I would hear his clothes rustle. I was overwhelmed with wonder and joy, and offered the purest worship of my life. I just wanted to stay there for ever, loving him. I was afraid that if I moved, the moment would be over, and yet, because it was so utterly unexpected and totally over-whelming, I knew it was more than my imagination. Jesus was there, and he loved me.

I don't know how long I stayed there, transfixed. I do know that from then on I never again doubted that Jesus looks upon his handicapped ones with compassion, and that we should pray for their healing.

Eventually, I just had to return to the noise of the chil-dren... but wonderfully, Jesus came too. The knowledge of his presence stayed with me, moving from room to room, watching over me as I fell asleep, and warming me when I woke. A special peace descended on the family, and I thought I would never lose patience with them again.

Then, inevitably I suppose, the day before the service I snapped at Richard and felt Christ's expression change to one of sadness, as his presence faded. I was distraught and cried out, 'Jesus, come back to me!' but I knew instinctively that he couldn't give me this special awareness of himself while I was angry.

It wasn't until the service itself that I felt again Christ's warming presence. With a few friends behind us in the Lady Chapel at our church I dropped to my knees at the altar between the two boys. As I did so, the awareness of Jesus' special presence returned. We were all anointed with oil, and received the laying on of hands. It was as if Jesus himself were touching me. After the service this awareness faded again, but this time I knew Jesus was looking at me with great compassion, and I didn't feel upset.

A few days after the service Audrey, my God-found friend, came round and gave me a chance to take stock of what had happened.

'I found the service very moving,' she began cautiously. 'I don't know what I expected to happen, but it sort of gave me hope.'

'Oh, me too,' I agreed. 'Somehow it didn't matter that nothing dramatic came out of it.' This gave her the lead for the question she hadn't dared to ask.

'Do you think there has been any improvement in the boys, then?'

I took a deep breath as I considered, and at that moment the boys rushed in like a hurricane.

'We want a drink too, Mummy,' said Richard, jealously eyeing our mugs of coffee.

'You can if you ask nicely,' I countered, pretending not to notice Audrey's amazement at his sentence structure.

'Please, Mummy,' he parroted at me. But what a wonderful clear sound. I was already putting two half mugs of orange and two biscuits on a tray.

'Good boy,' I conceded. 'You can have this on the

kitchen table. All right?'

'Yes, Mummy,' he chirped as he followed me. I smugly anticipated Audrey's reaction. She didn't disappoint me.

'Well,' she gasped on my return, 'I've never heard his consonants so clearly. And I'm sure that before he would have said, "Drink Richard too." I can't believe it. What's he like on longer sentences?'

'Well, we need a bit more work there,' I laughingly admitted. Her surprise was a wonderful joy to me. 'But I think you're right about the hope. That's what's really changed. I feel that I can correct him now, and that he can learn, instead of me letting him churn out words with no links which no one except the family can understand.'

'So what about Paul?' I heard the caution in Audrey's voice again.

'Well, that's more a question of my attitude changing, really. Nothing as obvious as Richard, I'm afraid. There is one thing though.' I paused. 'I don't really know how to say this – it sounds a bit dramatic....'

Audrey laughed. 'It's OK, I've got used to drama in this house.'

'Well, you know Paul has been having these screaming fits?' She nodded. 'I've tried everything – hugging, smacking, leaving him alone, even out-screaming him – and nothing works. He just goes on and on until he decides to stop. Well, we hadn't had one since the service, and I sort of hoped that they could have disappeared, because I've been looking for improvements, of course. Anyway, yesterday, off he goes again, and my heart was in my boots. Then I suddenly had the strong impression that I should pick him up and take him to his bed. It was quite a struggle, and I had dropped to my knees to put him down, when I felt I should stay there, with my hands on him, and ask Jesus to cast out Satan, because that's who was causing the screams.'

'Go on,' said Audrey, unperturbed. 'Did it work?'

'Yes... I think so. Not immediately, but it's the first time

I felt there was any connection between what I did and the screams stopping.' I smiled. 'Now I don't know whether I want him never to scream again, or to have another bout today so I can see whether it works!'

'You are amazing,' Audrey laughed with me.

I didn't feel amazing. Although I was so grateful to God for revealing himself to me in the way he had, and I was now seeing any bright side of the situation there was to be seen, I was always tired. Perhaps the greatest miracle was the way I kept going, and the way I went on praying. But there were so many encouragements.

Paul was terrified of dogs, and quite irrational about it. However far away it was, as soon as he spotted one he ran in the other direction. One day soon after the service we were coming back from the shops when suddenly a dog behind us, which I hadn't seen, caused Paul to shoot off the pavement across the road. A van was coming quite fast down the road, but I knew Paul wouldn't try to avoid it in any way, and he was beyond my reach. I screamed out loud, 'God, save him!'

Paul stopped abruptly, and the van missed him by inches. I was shaking from head to foot, and went down to the vicarage with Paul. The vicar was very concerned, called it 'a matter of life and death' and promised that all his staff would pray about this fear.

Two weeks later we saw preparations being made in our little park for the Roman Catholic Corpus Christi procession, and the children said they wanted to go. Although a crowd in a park often meant dogs, and a commotion there would be rather like disturbing church, I decided to risk it. Half way through the procession I realised there was a dog sitting right by Paul. He seemed totally unafraid.

On our way home I said to Paul, 'Do you know why you were not afraid of that dog? It was because Jesus was near you.' From then on whenever we saw a dog we would stop and I would get Paul to pray, 'Please Jesus take away my fear of dogs.' Soon he could pass without fear quite close to a dog, although for many years he reacted with some distress if a dog actually touched him. How I praised God for this healing. Even Alec admitted that it must have been God's work.

That summer, his fourth term, Paul really began to do well in school. Well for him, anyway. One day he came home wearing a Merit badge, because he had sung a song so beautifully that he had been taken to each class to sing it, and had been pleased with the other children's applause, which was a real step forward. He even began copying what the other children were doing in play. His teacher was so positive, but I suppose she felt it was neither kind nor necessary to state the obvious fact that he wasn't 'normal'. I began to lose my perspective on the matter... my hopes rose unjustifiably.

Thus I was quite shattered when a week before the end of their fourth term at school we received a letter from the County Education Officer notifying us that both Paul and Richard were to be excluded from school at the end of term. 'Suitable arrangements' would be made for their education. This seemed likely to take the form of a home teacher.

Paul was heart-broken when he realised he wasn't going back to school. Several times a day he would put on his hat and coat, climb onto my lap and sob, 'Go to school, go to school.' And week after week the promised teacher didn't arrive. Those days were so long.

When a Mrs Stemp arrived to take an hour with each of them every day, she found Paul very unco-operative, and soon more and more of Paul's hour was taken up with Richard, who loved his lessons. What Paul needed was not the teaching so much as the presence and play of other children around him, even if he didn't relate to them. He missed this terribly, and his behaviour became more and more difficult.

Alec's diary gave him a chance to express some of his

worries and to let off steam when the boys' behaviour got on top of him.

> *March 6th:* Una took both boys to mid-week Communion at church. Paul very badly behaved. He's so very bored without school and causes me much worry. He's just wasting mentally. He eats well and is very strong, but always difficult and fractious. Had to smack him for naughtiness in evening, hated having to do so.

> *March 11th:* Paul surly and fractious all day, as usual reaching a peak at bedtime. Tonight he up-ended his bed and climbed on top of his wardrobe, refusing to come down. It's so senseless, and so tiring.

> *March 12th:* Tonight the contents of his drawers were all over the floor. I started to sort them all out, but Una said to just straighten them into piles and she would put them back in the morning. How tired she looks.

On March 22nd, I had an interview with a Schools Medical Officer, who recommended that Richard should go to a Special School in September, and that steps should be taken towards Paul going to a Rudolf Steiner Curative School. How grateful I was that there was some hope of someone else taking over.

The next day Audrey looked after the children while Alec and I visited Mr Harding, the man our vicar had contacted about the healing ministry. He lived in the heart of such beautiful, peaceful countryside, that just to be there was a healing. He spent time with us teaching me how to relax: as I gradually wound down I was to say, 'Let go and let God.' From then on I tried to do this every day at home, and it was a great help to me, mentally, physically and spiritually. To cap the day, we got home and found all three children in bed asleep. Good old Audrey!

For some time Richard had been having headaches, and then sometimes he would become 'starey'. The doctor suggested epilepsy, and indeed as it developed the symptoms became more pronounced. There would be at least one day of migraine and sickness either side of the actual fit, so it meant several days of misery for the poor lad. By contrast with Paul he was so helpful. Again, Pips was in a completely different category, and seemed amazingly immune to the chaos that often surrounded her. I gave her as much time as I could, but it could never have been a normal childhood.

Alec wrote in his diary:

*May 14th:* This is the second day Paul has shut himself in his room and urinated all over the place. I gave him a good hiding, and I feel it may actually have some effect this time.

*June 21st:* Paul's cystitis is worse today, and he continues constipated which causes him a lot of distress. My stomach is still playing me up feeling bruised and sore, sometimes creasing me up with pain.

*July 2nd:* Confirmation from the County Education Officer that, provided Paul is accepted by the Rudolf Steiner school, the county will pay his fees for a trial period. Una said, 'Praise God.' I said, 'At last.' Any way you look at it, it's good news, but there's no sign of an appointment with the headmaster of the school, so who knows how long that will take?

Three days after Christmas a big swing arrived for Richard and Paul, a gift from the BBC appeal for handicapped children at home. It was a great success, and kept all the children occupied for many an hour. I was all the more grateful because apart from half a dozen close friends, there often seemed little sign that anyone 'out there' cared very much at all. It felt as though the walls were closing in on us.

# CHAPTER FOUR

Months passed. Richard reached ten, and Paul eight, and I still had them both at home. It seemed endless. Paul's latest obsession was with gas flames, so he had to be monitored carefully, and he also began picking holes in the plaster in the hall, a trait which had until then been confined to his bedroom. Now every weekend Alec had to spend making up plaster for the pockmarked hall. Another great irritation was that he developed a fear of taps running, and would scream 'off, off, off' until I had what I needed.

Everything seemed to be more and more of a struggle for me. On February 3rd, Alec wrote in his diary, 'Una very strung up and nervy with the strain of looking after the children.'

The next day I was in the kitchen with the children when suddenly their voices seemed to recede from me even though I could see them around me, and I felt as though I was going under an anaesthetic. I was just able to write on a piece of paper 'Babs, come, I'm ill' and send

Richard with it to a friend down the road.

Babs rushed over to find me very confused and so weak I could hardly move. She immediately sent for Alec, and Mrs Stemp who had arrived to teach Richard took him home with her for the day. Babs took Pips home with her. I lay on the divan, with just enough grip on reality to pray, 'Oh God, what can we do?' and then I thought of Audrey. Alec went over to see her and her husband Chris who was unemployed at the time, and they both agreed to help: Audrey in the house and Chris with the providing of dinner.

The doctor when he saw me said I was suffering from total physical and nervous exhaustion, and the only cure was complete rest. He arranged for us to have a Home Help under the council scheme.

By the end of that day practical matters seemed to be well in hand. Then in the evening our vicar came round with so much concern in his smile I found myself reassuring him that I would be fine in a week. Perhaps I thought that was realistic, but I was soon to learn otherwise. He prayed with me, and said all his church would be praying too. I felt reassured, because I couldn't have put two prayers together. I just wanted to be 'away from it all', and the obvious way to do that was to sleep.

It had always been difficult to express exactly how exhausting and unpredictable Paul could be, but poor Audrey soon began to find out. Here is her account of her first afternoon's walk.

The first walk, I had been aiming to take them near the station to see the trains. That walk was a nightmare with a capital N. We came up to a bus about ten seconds before the conductor rang the bell for the bus to move on. Paul jumped on and ran like lightning upstairs. I also jumped on, begging the conductor not to move off. On the pavement stood Richard screaming with panic and wee Pips by his side. I rushed upstairs and manhandled Paul – who was roaring with laughter – back down the stairs. He was stronger than I, so that took some effort. Needless to say, the conductor was complaining rather than helping and nearly letting the bus move on all the time. At last we were all standing together safely on the pavement.

Seconds later, the Nightmare started again. Just round the corner was the station café. Suddenly Paul had whipped in through the door and helped himself to several bars of chocolate from the counter. The lady assistant shouted at Paul and at me. I had just got the others in through the door. I tried to explain, but Paul just streaked out again, across the road through the thundering traffic and jumped clean over the fence into the railway yard. Thank goodness he stopped there, and that gave me the time to placate the assistant and make my way across the road with a yelling Richard and Pips, who couldn't keep up with the sudden changes in direction and kept crying plaintively, 'Wait for me, Auntie Audrey, wait for me!'

We stood looking over the fence at Paul, who was polishing off the chocolate at a prodigious speed, when a railway worker spotted our plight and manhandled Paul back over the fence. Paul thought the whole thing was a tremendous joke, and giggled to himself all the time, which increased my anger and frustration, but there seemed to be nothing to say, somehow. I knew it was a waste of time. I had learned one lesson though – I kept a firm hold on his arm all the way home.

After that little expedition I kept away from shops and buses and the railway on future walks. It was almost better if you didn't see anything interesting at all. One day we passed a cement mixer, which of course fascinated Paul in particular. We paused for a moment, Paul sidling nearer all the time, until he suddenly tried to climb into it, and I had to drag him away, the protests of the workman ringing in my ears.

'Little Audrey', less than five feet tall, needed superhuman strength to carry on day after day. I prayed for her while she was out, and she told me that helped. What she didn't tell me for years afterwards was that she would go home every evening and burst into tears.

After ten days our curate's wife called to say that some

33

of the mothers in our church 'Fellowship of Marriage' had volunteered to take the children out in the afternoons on a rota basis. They thought it would be better to go in pairs, which was realistic of them, and also took a burden of worry off me. Not that I didn't pray for them, anyway! I was so grateful for this help, as these mothers gave up prime time, rushing through their housework in the morning and giving me their free time in the afternoon before collecting their own children from school. Practical help like this is very costly, but so precious.

After another two weeks, Audrey started coming three days a week instead of five, and the couple of hours the church friends put in became even more essential. By evening I didn't know where to put myself with fatigue. Alec had taken over the washing, ironing and mending, and he too was looking pale and drawn.

It was a long haul up for all of us. It was like six weeks out of my life, but we were all learning so much about each other and ourselves. In all that time I had no particular experience of God, and many moments of frustration at my own weakness and the hopelessness of our situation, but I still saw God as the source of my healing. Vivid in my mind is the sheer delight of the lovely spring day when we went to Audrey's caravan in the woods and picked primroses. I felt as though I had been let out of prison.

The following day I felt well enough to go to a meeting in Southampton on autism. Someone had pointed it out to me and suggested that it might be interesting. When I went I had hardly heard the word 'autism' before, but as the talk proceeded I wanted to shout, 'Yes, that's it. You really do understand, don't you? You mean there are others like Paul?'

The speaker explained that an autistic child cannot relate to others, but lives in a world of his own. Nearly all mentally handicapped children can relate to, and communicate with, people to some degree. The autistic child,

34

however, is not only unable to comprehend language, but even the meaning of gestures. Whereas a normal baby will respond with pleasure to his mother's smile, an autistic baby will only see his mother screwing up her face in a peculiar way, and not understand at all the emotion behind it. As he grows, he totally fails to develop a normal bond with people, and as soon as he is physically independent, he wants to be alone. He is not unintelligent, but becomes retarded because he cannot assimilate information. His behaviour patterns are often bizarre and disturbing, probably fuelled by overwhelming frustration. Knowing this drained away some of my anger, but made me so sad.

Talking afterwards I found another mother who felt the same way. This new understanding didn't change my situation materially, but to have a label I could put on his condition took away some of the burden of guilt I carried at having such an unmanageable child. Perhaps one of the lessons I had learned from my collapse was that I needed help and shouldn't feel ashamed of the fact. I didn't have to spend my life atoning for the 'sin' of having produced Paul.

So it was that when the County Health Authorities arranged for the boys to go away for a fortnight before Easter, I was only too delighted, though worried. After three days a letter arrived from the Matron, and I slowly made myself a cup of tea before opening it with my heart bashing against my ribs.

> Dear Mrs Menniss,
> I know you must be wondering how Richard and Paul are: they are both quite settled and happy, and no trouble at all. It is obvious that they are children who are greatly loved. This is a Christian Home, and we all gather for prayers in the mornings.

I could read no more as my eyes filled with tears of

gratitude. Once again I felt vindicated in my belief that love and a faith in the essential dignity of both boys, despite their handicaps, could help them to have lives which had meaning. God has a place for such as them. It is our job to recognise that truth and act accordingly. Wishing they were different because it is all too much trouble is no help. Wishing them to be different for their own sake brings out the best in them. If you accept handicaps as part of a fallen creation, you must make room for handicapped people. Yet however well adjusted I became to my own sons, I couldn't control the reactions of others. This is why this letter was such a triumph. Someone else was taking the risk of believing that, even though they would never be anything very much in the eyes of men, they deserved a place in God's world.

Alec didn't share my feelings when I read the letter to him that evening. He was aware that I was disappointed by his reaction.

'What do you expect me to say, love? I'm glad they're having a good time and not running someone else ragged. I'm even gladder that you're getting a break. But that's the end of it, as far as I'm concerned.'

'Well, I was just thinking I would like to arrange for another healing service for them....' My voice tailed off uncertainly. How could I explain the inner conviction that this was what God wanted me to do, even if there was no rational basis for it?

'Oh, love,' Alec sighed. He reached across the table and put his hand over mine. 'I don't know if that's a very good idea.' Getting no response from me, he went on. 'You know how worked up you got about the last one, and how disappointed we were that they weren't healed. I don't want to see you put yourself through that again.'

I stared at him. Did he live in the same world as me?

'But I wasn't worked up, Alec, I was full of hope.'

'Yes, but where did it get you? Those boys aren't healed. There isn't any point.'

'Alec, I can't believe you're saying this. What about Richard's speech? What about the smile Paul sometimes gives now, and the patience he shows when things don't happen according to his timetable? Isn't that healing? You expected so much that you can't see what you did get. I'm not disappointed. I'm looking forward to what God wants to do next time.'

'Sorry, love. We see things differently. I can't stop you, so you go ahead. You'll just have to count me out.'

So I did, with a heavy heart. Again there were improvements to my eyes, but Alec was blinded to them. Even if there had been nothing I could put down as God's work I would still have done it, because I believed God was telling me to.

Meanwhile the schooling situation was clarifying. Richard was tested and found to have an IQ of 62. These IQs are now considered fairly arbitrary and meaningless, but in those days it was life and death to me, because under a certain IQ level, the authorities could deny any responsibility for a child's education. At around this time I was finally given a diagnosis for Richard's problems. It could have been a pre-natal cerebral haemorrhage, or else brain damage during birth. Once again, this information was vital, and yet had no impact on me at all. There was nothing to be done about the past. I had to accept him, love him and fight for his future. I was very happy when within a month a boarding place became vacant at a special school. Yet this was the first time one of my children had left home, and parting with him was a difficult moment for everyone.

Alec's diary sums it up. 'Richard was very brave until the actual leaving, then cried a lot. Pips cried, then Una, and I felt numb.'

Probably Paul showed no interest at all, but then he had only just learnt to say 'Hello' when Alec came home from work. We were used to living with an emotional black hole.

37

We visited Richard several times in the first term. He got off to a bad start because he couldn't wash and dress in the ten minutes that the boys were allocated for this in the mornings. I felt guilty because it looked for a while as though I had misled them about his competence in these areas, but then I felt defiant. Ten minutes! Was this a school for backward boys or a military establishment? However, things blew over before relationships became strained, and Richard seemed settled and happy.

Sometimes I was grateful for the relief it was to have him at school, but I often felt guilty as though I were washing my hands of my own son. Was this the only possible way forward for Paul as well?

# CHAPTER FIVE

In the absence of spaces at the nearest Rudolf Steiner School, Paul had been put down for a place at the Steiner school in Aberdeen. There seemed some chance this would come up quite soon, which was a great relief as his main interests at the time were gas flames and opening the washing machine when it was working.

At last, over the summer, we had a letter saying that Paul could start at Aberdeen in September. We were delighted and accepted by return of post.

The very next day came a quite different letter from the County Education Officer saying that we should take no action concerning the vacancy as they were reconsidering the whole question of whether the fees should be paid by the County in the circumstances. It was they who had first made the suggestion of the Rudolf Steiner School, and had twice stated in writing that they would pay, so we protested vigorously. They answered that Aberdeen was too far away. We replied that it hadn't moved since their last offer to help, when Aberdeen had been suggested. It looked as though someone had over-stepped the mark and then been overruled.

We wrote and had interviews with various people, the vicar wrote, the Social Services wrote, even our MP appealed – all in vain. With four days to go to the start of term, Alec's parents lent us the money for one term's fees, and I could start to plan our journey to Myrtle House, the Rudolf Steiner School in Aberdeen.

Richard and Pips had started their terms already, so when Audrey asked if she could come to help and say goodbye to Paul, I looked forward to an enjoyable, relaxing day. I made coffee, and we sat in the late sunshine enjoying the blaze of colour from my chrysanthemums. Then, suddenly, I realised Paul had gone. When we didn't find him on foot, friends started out on bikes, and at this point Audrey really had to get home before her own son returned from school. She set off for the bus, promising to phone when she got back. By this time there were people in and out of the house and going off in all directions looking for Paul. Half an hour later, the phone rang.

'Una, dear, this is Audrey. You'll never guess what – I've got Paul!' Stunned silence. 'Are you all right?'

'Yes, I'm fine, but....'

'Well, there I was sitting on the bus and we were most of the way home, when I suddenly glimpsed Paul walking along the side of the road. I jumped off at the next stop, and he said, "Going to Auntie Audrey's caravan." He nearly made it as well! No, I don't know how he got across all those busy roads. Oh well, I'm phoning from a petrol station. Paul's fine, he's just having some chocolate. Anyway, there's a man here offering to bring us back. I'll be with you in ten minutes, I should think. You'd better put the kettle on. You sound as though you need it!'

Dear Audrey had done it again.

After that, we doubled our precautions about the trip to Aberdeen. Alec came with us as far as King's Cross, and we brought with us two sturdy belts attached by a longer leather strap. When we were safely in the compartment, Paul and I were strapped together to prevent any escape.

A kind sailor shared the compartment with us, and when night came helped us to find comfortable sleeping positions along the seat. Amazingly Paul slept until six o'clock. We had sandwiches for breakfast, Paul drinking most of the orange juice I had packed. The sailor got off at Edinburgh, but dashed back with a cup of tea for me – bless him! From then on the train stopped at every station, and each time Paul tried to get off, saying, 'Go to school, go to school.' Eventually we reached Aberdeen, and got a taxi. At last Paul's dream was being fulfilled.

And so was mine. As I stepped inside Myrtle House I was overwhelmed by a sense of peace, both in the house itself and in myself, feeling immediately that this was the right place for Paul. The atmosphere was calm, and homely, not like an institution at all. He went off very happily, and I had a talk with Matron, who was called Nina. She seemed to understand intuitively the mixture of sadness and relief I felt on parting. We both felt I shouldn't say good-bye formally, but I looked through a glass door at Paul playing happily and went away feeling very relieved and reassured.

My train wasn't due for some hours, so I went back into Aberdeen and had a meal with a cup of coffee. Then, as I walked around some back streets, I suddenly felt terribly ill, and was nearly knocked down crossing a road. Looking for somewhere quiet, I went to a churchyard, and then into the church. I hoped to recover somehow, but as I prayed in the church, the word 'hospital' was written before my eyes. Outside again, I asked a lady if there was a hospital near, and indeed the Aberdeen Royal Infirmary was only a quarter of a mile away. I couldn't have walked much further.

The receptionist there told me to join the queue of people waiting on the red plastic covered chairs, but I nearly collapsed as she spoke, and I was ushered to a room by a sister and nurse who were concerned to learn how far from home I was, and of the journey I had yet to make. A sympathetic doctor arrived and after a few words with me asked for a large jug of water and told me to drink and drink. I was dehydrated! In twenty-four hours of high stress, I had only had one cup of tea and one of coffee. I was so relieved it was something so simple, but felt rather silly. The nurse put me at my ease, and even more wonderful, said she had friends working at Myrtle House and she knew Paul would have wonderful loving care. With the sleeping tablet they gave me I slept all the way back to King's Cross, and arrived home refreshed, overwhelmed with a sense of God's love, and nearly walking on air.

'Don't forget, love, that we've still got a battle on our hands over those fees.' Alec, who never got as excited or as depressed as I did, obviously felt he had to bring me back down to earth with a note of caution.

'I don't want to think about that yet, Alec. Why not enjoy what we've got? Everything is wonderful. It'll all work out somehow.'

Life seemed very quiet with both Richard and Paul away, and I tried to devote more time to Pips. She seemed very reluctant to appreciate my efforts, and I had to accept that she had of necessity developed a highly in-dependent spirit.

It was, however, good to have the worry taken from me, once we had a few letters from both schools to assure us that things were running smoothly. Alec wrote weekly to both boys, and illustrated his letters with drawings. Richard could read his own letters, and Paul's nursery parents would read his to him, and show him the photo-graphs of family, friends and familiar places which they suggested we send. It was so thoughtful of the school to think of this, as it would have been very disheartening to feel we were being forgotten. I certainly never forgot them for more than an hour at a time.

Paul's school suggested that he should stay there for Christmas, and although Richard came home for two weeks and we decorated a tree, I couldn't feel quite right without Paul there. We soon heard from Nina, the Matron, that he was making rapid improvements in his behaviour and that he had enjoyed Christmas very much. All the staff hoped that he would be able to stay.

'So do we!' I wanted to shout. The County, however, appeared immovable over the issue of the fees. At one interview it was reiterated that Aberdeen was too far away. I rather acidly repeated my answer that it hadn't moved since the original offer was made, but the official said it would be difficult to supervise Paul at such a distance. I later discovered that there was someone whose job it was to supervise the school on behalf of children sent by English Education Committees. Our MP agreed to take up our case with the Minister of Education, and he also had a conversation with our vicar, Canon Lambert, who never ceased to champion our cause. We soon learned, however, that a Minister of Education could not overrule the decision of a County Education Committee. We approached the Ministry of Pensions on the grounds that Alec received a disability pension – in vain. We began to face the fact that we might always have to pay for Paul.

After we felt we had left no stone unturned, we had gained just a quarter of the year's fees between my brother and the Royal Tank Regiment Benevolent Fund. Alec's parents could advance the difference, but we had to work out how we could ever repay them. Our modest living standard had to come down several notches. Cast-off clothing became the norm, and I so regularly visited a second-hand clothing stall at the local market that the owner got to know our sizes and put items aside for my next visit!

Richard's school report at Easter revealed that he was often teased by the other boys, and that his fits were increasing in regularity, but that he was sociable and very appreciative of things done for him. I noticed quite a change in him when he came home: he seemed more mature, but slightly withdrawn. We did as many fun things as we could on our budget, like picking primroses in the woods, and my spirits were given a further lift to enjoy such beauty with him. Paul was not to come home, so we decided we had to go to him, even though it would mean a journey of three days to get there.

I steeled myself against lack of reaction from Paul. 'I must not let it hurt,' I told myself over and over again. When we arrived, he was so excited and pleased to see us that I nearly wept. And he was so much more manage-able. When I shouted 'Stop!', he actually stopped. On the beach he allowed Pips to play near him, instead of shout-ing, 'Pips, go away.' We watched him at a party where he was obviously enjoying himself.

Perhaps most amazing of all, I watched him at a kind of service in the chapel. It was candle-lit, and a lyre was playing, so that the peace and simplicity seemed to hold all the children. There were worship songs, simple prayers, a gospel reading and a short talk about how we are in this world to help one another. Each child was taken by the hand and told, 'The Spirit of the Lord will come to you if you seek him,' and the child answered, 'I will seek him.'

I was very moved by this, and although I realised that Rudolf Steiner was not a Christian, nothing I saw or heard contradicted the Bible. Certainly the improvement in Paul bore testimony to the fact that the trust they placed in these difficult children was bearing fruit.

At first, I discovered, they had had great problems with Paul. Piet, a junior houseparent, had been quite unable to cope, and Paul had been transferred to the care of Gus-tav, who nearly admitted defeat as well. The matter came before their 'Council', who called Paul in and said that if he didn't start being good immediately, he would have to leave the school. This approach worked.

We were told about the technique which they used at the school for dealing with Paul, and they asked us to use it when we took him home. In practical terms this meant outlining to him what we wanted, and then giving him a choice. For example, if he picked up what he was doing and put it in the cupboard as asked, he could have bubbles in his bath. If he didn't, he wouldn't. The trick was to find something that made it worth his while. Often it was easier to outline a punishment, such as missing an outing, for not complying. We thought this worth trying.

Previously, there was always trouble to get Paul into the car to go home, and he hated having his hand held. During our time together I explained to him, 'Paul, it's time to go to the car now. If you walk nicely, I won't hold your hand, but if you run away I shall have to. Which is it to be?'

He replied, 'Walk nicely to the car,' and did so. This to me was unbelievable progress.

Altogether, the huge effort of the trip north was made worthwhile by the knowledge that Paul was happy and accepted, and now I could imagine him in his daily life. He would come home for the summer, and there was a good chance that he could be transferred to our local Rudolf Steiner School so the Education Authority would be persuaded to pay his fees.

For a few brief weeks things looked fine and settled. Sports Day and Open Day at Richard's school soon blew this apart. I asked Richard's teacher how he was progressing, and she replied, 'Well, you've seen his books. You can see for yourself how badly he is doing.' It transpired that his IQ had been retested and had come out at 44. He would have to leave at the end of term, and with such a low IQ the County could repudiate any further responsibility for his education.

I had been in this pit before. Why did it always hurt so much? Would I ever get used to it? Why did one of the boys always seem to pull me down when the other was doing so well? It was the see-saw of emotions which was so exhausting. Perhaps it would have been better never to have hoped. In the state I now was, I would probably undo all the training Paul had received from the Rudolf Steiner School.

By contrast, we had an almost conciliatory interview with the County Education Authority. They expressed their admiration at the way we had struggled, and said they would pay for Paul's place at the nearest Rudolf Steiner School if he performed well in an IQ test they would do at the end of the summer. I prayed for guidance about how to treat him, and the answer took the form of a letter from his house-mother, Gerda, giving very helpful suggestions.

So Paul's situation was now really very good, and it was Richard who caused the heartbreak. I prayed with little conviction – indeed it even crossed my mind that if I stopped praying, Satan would leave me and the boys alone. But somehow, Satan usually just oversteps the mark, and I recognised him as the source of that particular idea. Anyway, how could I do other than turn to God, when I knew I was only being kept from mental and spiritual breakdown by the assurance that 'underneath are the everlasting arms'? It was as natural as breathing to me – and as necessary.

# CHAPTER SIX

The promised IQ test on Paul was a disaster: result 38. The doctor agreed that he had improved socially a great deal, and that he was obviously at the right school, but there was no way the County would pay the fees given such a low intelligence.

That evening Alec set out for his parents' house, and they agreed to advance the money on the understanding that we would pay them back as fast as we could. Since we were already counting pennies, this was a burden both to Alec, who worked as much overtime as he could, and to me, who actually had to make the budget stretch. As long as we could see what a great improvement there was in Paul, it all seemed worth it, but the bad days were very bad, and those summer holidays were long.

At home with nothing to distract and entertain him, Paul could be horrible. A momentary lapse of concentration on my part could make hours of work for me. One dinner-time I put the ketchup on the table instead of mounting guard over it, and returned from fetching my

47

own plate to find Paul's food swamped with red. There followed a tussle with the bottle, during which the table-cloth was liberally splotched. After a smack, Paul calmed down, but later deliberately damaged the tablecloth with his fork while pretending to clear it up.

Later that day, I left Paul with a jigsaw puzzle while I put Pips to bed, and came down to find bits of jigsaw stuffed and bent down the side of the armchair, while the dining room cushions were rammed into the grate. Most children are capable of this sort of thing, I suppose, but not with such regularity and wanton destructiveness.

And of course damage has a price tag on it, either in money or in effort to restore the situation. You can save money in lots of little ways if you have time and energy to spare, but during that summer I had little of either. When I caught sight of myself in a mirror I realised that I looked permanently tired, pale and worried.

Perhaps this is why certain lovely summer treats stand out in my mind. Our favourite seaside place was definitely Studland Bay: the sea was very shallow and good for paddling. There was also a derelict jetty with criss-crossed metal struts – a perfect climbing frame for Paul, who was off like a shot. He couldn't read the big notice saying DANGER KEEP OFF!

I had a choice. I could start shouting at him, arguing, chasing, maybe even climbing after him, then moving all our bags far enough away to hope he would forget the jetty, and even after that watching him all day to make sure he hadn't done a disappearing trick. Or I could 'not see' the notice and have an hour's peace in the sun. No contest. We even took a photo of him high up with his foot resting unwittingly on the notice!

At lunch-time the sandwiches were the only magnet required to extricate him. Once the tide dropped in the afternoon there were lovely shallow pools full of the glories that all children insist on taking home with them.

There were several good trips like that over the course

of the holidays, especially when Alec took a week off. To go away to sleep was out of the question, but we made several interesting forays to various spots, and I was pleased that we so seldom had trouble with Paul. Sometimes, however, we did have to resort to smacks, which I always felt to be a great failure according to the principles laid down by his school.

Although I had been very impressed with the success of their 'choice' method, it took a while to explain to Paul the consequences of his choice. If he decided not to hear, he had already made his decision (usually the wrong one) by the time you had mapped out what you were going to say, and you found yourself shouting complicated instructions to an unheeding and rapidly vanishing back.

One factor which always controlled us was the reaction of others to our strange little group. Often we headed for the less-favoured areas of the wood, beach or town just so that we wouldn't be noticed. With no information, an onlooker would either see two extremely difficult boys or, even worse, a behaviour pattern which was disconcertingly strange. Many was the time Paul would get his 'dance-step' fixation – walking backwards and forwards several times before going on – when there were people behind us.

If I was feeling sensitive, there was no reaction they could show without hurting me. They stared, and I felt awful, my cheeks burning. They pretended not to notice, and I felt ignored, invisible, angry. Occasionally, if Alec weren't in sight, someone would offer help. But how could I show any gratitude? There was nothing they could do. There was no quick explanation to what was going on, and they didn't really want a medical lesson, or my life history. In my embarrassment I probably answered rather sharply. The isolation of handicap is an ever-renewable pain.

Richard caused me more irritation than embarrassment. He developed a whiney way of talking which really

49

got under my skin, and sometimes repeated meaningless phrases over and over again. 'Jimmy Cross, Jimmy Cross, Jimmy Cross, Jimmy Cross...' was awful if it went on for one minute, but ten minutes later I was at screaming pitch. Yet had he done anything wrong? Worst of all was the knowledge that he had no school to go to at the end of the holidays, and I couldn't even tell myself, 'Only another two weeks....'

Like Paul, Richard was better when he had more attention, because a child like him who has little motivation and imagination is quickly bored. He never found anything to do by himself, and needed constant stimulation. He fared better when Paul returned to school two weeks ahead of Pips, every piece of clothing packed with a prayer that we could continue to afford the fees.

Overall the improvement in Paul was quite marked: a smack now had some effect, and was needed far less often. Most noticeable was his increased ability to relate to people, to show us affection and to relate generally to the world around him. To our relief his transfer to the school at Ringwood had materialised, and we no longer had to plan long journeys in order to see him. I prayed that he would accept a change of school, and the warm atmosphere of the new school seemed to envelop him immediately. We were able to leave him without any qualms.

In the two weeks of Pips' holiday which remained we had several outings which were more restful for his absence. Now Richard's problems came to the fore, because Pips was less able to control her irritation when he became silly, and there was a lot of bickering. I couldn't help wondering whether Pips returned to school with a sigh of relief that she didn't have to be associated with these 'misfits' any longer. Certainly she seemed determined to conform, appear neat and tidy, and work hard, and this was bringing results which were gratifying to both her and her parents.

Sometimes I allowed myself to wonder just how easy life would be if all my children had turned out as I had anticipated. It was unimaginable, like guessing what you would be like if you had married someone else. Most of the time, of course, idle speculation was impossible: I was either 'on duty' or asleep.

Yet there was another level to my life, a constant reaching out to God in prayer. Sometimes I was asking for help – for wisdom, strength, patience, or ideas for something to do. But beyond that, often wordlessly, an awareness of God's love flowed through me, upholding me, transforming what I saw, and refreshing my spirit. If I ever wished things were different, I was brought up short by the thought that I might have not known God so intimately if I hadn't been so aware of my need.

I found it quite difficult that I could share none of this with Alec, but at least the children usually responded well to being in church, and often hummed or even sang canticles which they remembered. One afternoon when I was feeling quite low, Richard suddenly sang in perfect tune, 'The Lord God is our refuge, a very present help in trouble.' If an angel is a messenger from God, then he was an angel at that moment!

Naturally my chief concern that autumn was Richard's education. With Mrs Stemp's individual attention he had learnt to write fairly legibly, but at school this had been quite lost. Determined not to allow this backwards step, I set writing exercises which rapidly improved the situation, and with the acquisition of a 'Diary' notebook he became quite proficient at expressing what he had been up to. Often he was able to write that he had helped me – washing up, hoovering, cutting off dead flowers in the garden, or collecting blackberries and making bramble jelly. Since he needed constant supervision this was far more time-consuming than undertaking the jobs myself, but my campaign was not for a perfectly tidy house, which would have been self-defeating anyway, but for recognition of Richard's potential. It seemed to me that love should believe the best of everybody, and help them to live up to it: giving hope by having hope.

In this cause, I arranged for a local doctor to come to see some of his work and re-test his IQ. My apparent reason was that the test he had failed so abysmally at school had been done without notifying us, and it was therefore invalid. I demanded a re-test. If I had to appear belligerent, then so be it. Surely anyone could see that he could read quite well, better than some pupils at secondary school. The doctor couldn't deny this, and said he needed something much better than an Occupation Centre for the Mentally Handicapped, but that his reading ability counted for nothing with the County, who obviously had no intention of providing that 'something better'.

Paul's school contacted us a few days later to say that his 'fixations' were much worse, and he wasn't eating well. Eva Sachs, one of his teachers, suggested that he should come home for a few days.

This was quite a success at first, but Paul had one or two disturbing episodes of violence, throwing cutlery at Pips and Richard. Pips had a nasty cut on her forehead, and everyone was shaken by what happened. I decided I should let the school know about this when he returned to them, although I didn't want them to stop trusting him. It seemed that he was no further trouble there, though, because when I telephoned him on his birthday he burst out in a very excited voice, 'Hullo, Mummy. I've been a good boy!'

Back at home the Menniss family in general were struggling through coughs, colds, headaches, stomach pains and broken nights. The winter seemed unfailingly to bring us to our knees not just once, but over and over again. Several times over the winter we knocked at the door marked 'Schooling for Richard'. Pips' teacher very kindly allowed her to bring home old school books for him when she knew what the situation was, and his reading was improving all the time. The difficulty was knowing what to do with him once the 'lesson' part of the day was over. The lack of occupation drove him silly, so he would start jumping up and down and yelping, or displaying some other meaningless behaviour which outweighed all the goodwill he had built up over the few hours since the last episode.

Paul came home for the Easter holidays which, to begin with at least, were dominated by Richard's bad behaviour, as Alec's diary shows:

> Took family for picnic on Weston shore. On return, Richard threw a paddy because Una would not read to him. Repeated meaningless phrases over and over again with much gibberish and jumping up and down, acting generally wildly, biting fingers and trying various annoyances.

Worse was to come, and quite unexpectedly. Paul was told there were no more second helpings one dinnertime. He started jumping about, knocked over his drink, screwed up his face, spat, cried and punched Pips. Poor Pips was terrified, and the only way I could control him eventually was to sit on him on the floor. All this sparked off Richard's silly behaviour, and I felt as though I would go mad as well.

The next morning, Sunday, I very much wanted to go to church, but felt that Alec would resent me leaving him with the children, so I took them all with me. If ever there was a test of my belief that church calmed them, this was it. Once again, they were fine. I never found any reason for their consistently good behaviour in church, but I was so grateful.

Over this period, the County changed their tune a little, but only to the extent of finding another reason not to help with Paul's fees. The label 'mentally deficient' round his neck was replaced by another saying 'ineducable through mental health'. Given what I was coping with at home, my appeal against that judgement lacked conviction. I made it, nonetheless.

Richard was once again visited by an educationalist. He read very well to her, but she said he read without understanding because he couldn't repeat from memory what he had read. I pointed out that he could answer questions on the passage, but this apparently carried no weight with the doctor. Next I wrote some quite complicated instructions down, and he followed them to the letter. This had no effect either, and by this time I had quite resigned myself to not understanding what she meant by 'reading with understanding'.

Repeated letters to the County with additional – to my mind incontrovertible – evidence of Richard's capacity, had no effect. Then towards the end of the summer term we visited Paul at his school and later had tea with his teacher Eva Sachs. She was very concerned to hear what we were trying to cope with in connection with Richard and suggested that when we went on holiday to Bristol we should visit Dr Sahlman, the medical officer of the Rudolf Steiner Schools, who lived in the area.

This we did, and were quite amazed when this doctor not only offered us advice on how to handle him, but said she would find him a place at the Sheiling Rudolf Steiner School at Ringwood, where Paul was, if we could find the funds. It sounded like the same old story again, but she suggested that since we had both been in the forces we should approach the Soldiers', Sailors' and Airmen's Association. My heart sank at the thought of grovelling again.

'But you're not doing this for yourself,' she insisted. 'You're doing it for Richard. He's wasting his potential at the moment, and you can see what the frustration is doing to him.'

Certainly his fits were happening with increasing regularity. At least twice over the summer holidays he fell down apparently unconscious while we were out walking in the country, and was still for two or three minutes before coming round, getting up and walking off as if nothing had happened.

Tension was mounting between Alec and me over Richard's schooling. We both felt reluctant to beg for more money, and Alec was so desperate for peace he even talked of swapping Richard for Paul at the Sheiling School. As I prayed, however, I suddenly felt that I should do as the Rudolf Steiner doctor, Dr Sahlman, had suggested, and go and see Mrs Piggott, the local representative of the Soldiers', Sailors' and Airmen's Association. She was most sympathetic and promised to put our appeal for help forward to various Forces' charities. I filled in a form with detailed particulars of our income and expenditure, with the information that we were already paying Paul's fees, and borrowing money to do so.

Seeing it all in black and white could have made me more gloomy, but somehow it had the opposite effect: a sense of peace came over me. As I walked home I handed the whole matter over to God. Alec was so sure that nothing would come of it that I stopped talking about my conviction and my hope, but I thanked God daily from that time on.

Term started again for Paul after the summer, and my hope of Richard starting with him seemed to have come to nothing. Pips' term started as well, and I rather half-heartedly thought about planning lessons for Richard. Although I had not said anything to Alec, I had believed the need for this was over.

Then, on the morning I told myself that I really must begin some kind of teaching programme for Richard, the miracle letter arrived. The WRNS Benevolent Trust would pay three-quarters of the fees and the British Legion and the Royal Tank Benevolent Fund would make up the balance.

In a state of great joy I wrote to Dr Sahlman, who got through the necessary procedures in two weeks, and said they could take Richard whenever he was ready to come. In reckless mood I borrowed yet more money from Alec's parents and rushed into Southampton to buy some new clothes for Richard and some name tapes. Alec sewed these on with great willingness!

By October 4th we were ready to take Richard to the Rudolf Steiner Sheiling School. He was to live with Paul and ten other boys in Watchmoor Cottage where he was under the care of a housemother called Leonie.

Paul was pleased to see us all, Richard was happy to be left, and I thought I would burst with contentment. At his previous school Richard had been occupied, but not to much profit, whereas I knew that at the Sheiling School both boys would not only be given meaningful tasks, but loving care and understanding as well. I couldn't resist singing on the way home, while Alec smiled happily at my happiness. I wanted so much to tell him that God had fulfilled his promise, but I knew it would just sound like 'I told you so', and an argument now would spoil everything.

So I just sang, and the sun shone, and Alec smiled. I thought God was smiling too.

# CHAPTER SEVEN

It was time to take stock. After so many years of constant struggling with the boys, with money, with the educational bureaucracy, I hardly knew who I was. Now I could spend some time relating to my husband and daughter, and building up some kind of more normal life, at least during term time. Yet I wasn't ready yet to make lots of resolutions and plans: I just needed to take it easy.

For me, this took the form of bottling our bumper crop of apples and pears, picking blackberries and stocking up with local honey, which we loved. I spent hours in our garden. It was a corner plot, and therefore quite a bit larger than most in the road. The peace I felt there, the sense of harmony and working together with God, was just the respite I needed.

Alec, meanwhile, set himself various jobs around the house. Ever since we had moved in after our marriage he had been working at one DIY project after another: it was a hobby, I suppose, but it often seemed to me to border on obsession. Now, with less people around, he felt he could tackle the landing, stairway and hall. He always went in for meticulous preparation, and of course stripping down made the most horrific mess, but he had been wanting to do it for so long, I tried not to clear up around him too much. It was good to see him without the deep creases lining his face, and to sense a new lightness in his step, despite his artificial leg.

At the weekends when the weather was good he would join me outside, making crazy-paving slabs for paths. He wasn't so interested in getting his hands earthy, but I felt that we were working together in our different ways. We didn't talk a lot as we worked, but it was a companionable silence. Sometimes I found myself looking across at him, full of gratitude for his emotional strength. I could never have survived this far without him. Physically, however, he was far from strong, and I often wished he wouldn't exhaust himself as he did with his self-imposed labour. It must have satisfied his creative urge as gardening did mine, but he often suffered from stomach pains and made himself work on through them.

That autumn I joined the Southampton Society for Mentally Handicapped Children, feeling that I wanted to help others. Needless to say I was far too keen, and was elected to the Committee at the first meeting. Alec supported me in this as well, using his draftsman's skills to produce posters when necessary.

Our wedding anniversary that year really seemed to be celebrating a relationship which had grown threadbare and was now renewed. We couldn't afford any great celebrations, but we did splash out to the extent of mushrooms in the supper, followed by cherries and cream.

When the boys came home at Christmas, I wondered how it would feel to be a family again. Perhaps because they were getting over chicken pox, they were rather difficult, and Paul, thwarted in an attempt to run away, lay in the road and screamed. A policeman helped us to frog-march him back to his room, and with heavy hearts we arranged for him to go back to school only half-way through the holidays.

Once he had more of my attention, Richard was really quite a pleasure to be with. We did a lot of bird-spotting with his Christmas binoculars, and he was soon quite expert at picking out unusual birds. His triumphs included a spotted flycatcher, a stonechat and – joy of joys – a lesser-spotted woodpecker on our very own apple tree. I felt very reassured about him, and he settled back at school again with Paul, who had also been very reasonable, according to the staff.

As spring arrived, I realised that my clothes were getting very bad. I didn't have a single dress that wasn't beginning to look shabby. Was this something I could pray about? Recently I had started going to prayer meetings and had consciously widened the scope of my intercessory prayer, feeling guilty that my prayers were always so family-centred. Did God care what I looked like? I compromised. 'Lord, could you just provide one nice dress for me?'

A few days later I received a letter from my Uncle Harold, with whom I didn't have a lot of contact. He wrote, 'Denis [my brother] has just been in and told me about your difficulties, so I thought this cheque might come in useful.' Enclosed was a cheque for £5. Thank you, Lord! I bought a lovely dress in a sale, which left enough money to buy a pair of much needed trousers for Alec. Pips wanted nothing more than her Brownie uniform for her enrollment which was imminent. We had been saving for this, and now we could actually go out and buy it. How much pleasure that gift had brought, and what an encouragement to me. I knew God always heard me, and that he provided strength, hope, patience and lots of other things I was constantly running out of, but this money was so tangible – a special sign that God really cared.

In term time we kept in contact as much as possible with

the boys, taking them out for picnics some weekends, and writing to them. The school was very good at making them write to us, and we really looked forward to their letters, though Paul's were usually drawings with 'Love from Paul' at the bottom. As the summer holidays approached, however, we began to hear murmurs of trouble from the school about Paul. He didn't want to leave when we collected both of them for the holidays, and the staff said we could ring and arrange to have him brought back at any time, as we had done before. It was good to know we had that to fall back on, but I really didn't want to fail in this way again.

For the first two weeks, we were constantly at the point of taking him back, but always hopeful that today would be better. We were soon worn down, however, by his wakefulness at night, which kept us all up, often until three o'clock, and we felt this couldn't continue. For the sake of the others we decided to take him back. I felt torn in two, but that summer holiday was great fun, and by the end I was reassured that we had made the right decision.

A few days after Richard had returned to school, we received a letter. From the postmark I deduced it was from the boys, but on seeing the headed notepaper and typed lines I reached for a chair and sat down slowly as I skimmed through as far as Eva Sachs' signature. Then, not believing what I had seen, I read the middle paragraphs again.

Unfortunately, Paul has developed a new obsession with the railway track which borders part of our grounds. On several occasions he has slipped away and climbed over a high fence on to the track, where he wanders around aimlessly. Yesterday we found him a matter of minutes before the train went through. We have alerted the local railway station of the possibility of a boy being on the track at that point, but they reasonably replied that while they would warn their drivers, a train cannot stop very quickly and they can take no responsibility should an accident occur.

Obviously, my staff will do all they can to contain him, but I feel it is necessary to inform you of the situation. I'm afraid that unless he can change his behaviour patterns Paul will have to leave the school.

My heart sank. Had it all been too good to be true? No, surely this would pass like any other hiccup in Paul's life. Please, God.

It was not to be. Within a couple of weeks, Paul had got loose again, and while a tall member of staff scooted after him, Richard jumped up and down in anguish, screaming, 'My brother not get killed, my brother not get killed!' Paul was lying between the lines when they reached him, and had to be manhandled home for a massive sedative injection. The staff decided that the effect on the other boys, and Richard in particular, made it necessary for him to leave the school immediately. He must be fetched home tomorrow.

Alec and I were at rock bottom: we knew we couldn't contain Paul long in such a disturbed state. In the next few days we contacted the mental health people, our doctor, Alec's personnel officer, the probation officer – anyone who might be able to help. Paul was absolutely wild a lot of the time, and very noisy at night despite the sleeping pills. We were frantic. Without the intensive support of a few friends, and the prayers of the church, I don't know what we would have done.

After five days, it was decided that Paul could go to a unit for disturbed children, and a member of their staff, with a Mental Welfare Officer, arrived to collect us by car. I was glad to look round the bungalow he would be sharing with thirty other children and to see that it looked like a caring place. My relief at offloading him was completely outweighed by the guilt of this failure and the fear of the unknown future. Were there any further depths to which Paul's condition could sink?

I cried out to God in agony of mind, pleading for some

hope. Then, suddenly, I remembered the Minnie Louise Haskins poem.

> I said to the man who stood at the gate of the year, 'Give me a light that I may tread safely into the unknown.' And he replied, 'Go out into the darkness and put your hand into the hand of God' ... So I put my hand into the hand of God and he led me towards the hills and the breaking of day in the lone East.

Only a few weeks before I had seen just that, peeping out of the tent on our Derbyshire camping holiday. I looked to the East. Rays of light shone from behind a peak, and these grew stronger and brighter until the sun rose and flooded the valley with light. Now I dared to hope that one day in the future, if I kept my hand in the hand of God, the sun would come out again in our lives.

Our first visit to Paul was reassuring in as far as he seemed to have accepted that he now had a 'new school', but it made me realise that we had taken another downwards step: he was to have no education or training there. Most of the children in the unit were disturbed like Paul, but their intelligence was normal, so schooling was provided for them. Not so for Paul. He was retarded as well as disturbed, and couldn't be integrated in the same way. It made me feel that in the authorities' eyes he was the lowest of the low, although the staff when I met them were all very supportive. They had discovered that if he were allowed to wander around the grounds, he knew instinctively when a meal was due, and always turned up on time!

As always, we kept in touch regularly with both boys, so it was an appalling shock on our next visit to Paul to be intercepted at the door by the charge nurse and sidetracked into his office. To my amazement he started talking to Pips, asking her what sort of games she liked to play, and would she like to go and find a jigsaw with a nurse? I smiled reassuringly at her as she went off, a very composed but wary eight-year-old, while inside me my heart turned to ice. I couldn't trust myself to speak, and in the few seconds it took for the charge nurse to arrange his thoughts I went to hell and back.

'We thought it would be better for Phillipa not to see Paul today, because he's under heavy sedation. There's been a bit of an accident, you see. He jumped through a window and cut his abdomen on the glass. We've had to put some stitches in, and of course they won't heal if he runs around, so we've got to keep him very quiet. Do go and see him, but I must warn you that it's possible that he won't recognise you.'

As we tiptoed into the room, I thought I had never seen such a grey face. A nurse sat beside him, trying not to intrude on this difficult moment. I forced my face to smile for me, and mouth 'Hello' at her. After a few seconds' anxious scanning of my son's lifeless features, I tried again. 'Is he asleep?' I said, a little louder. But this roused him and he struggled to open his heavy eyelids. He focused on the nurse, and in a slurred voice said, 'Wanna get up.'

Deftly, she straightened out the elbow onto which he was trying to push himself up, and said, 'Not just now, there's a good boy. Lie still. Your mum and dad have come to see you.' I took a few steps forward and smiled brightly.

'Hello, Paul. I hear you've had a bit of an accident.' His smile as he recognised my voice turned my numb fear into searing pain. 'My son, my son. How can I help you? Why is your life such a mess? Why can't my love lift you out of this? Why is it always you?' My knees buckled just as Alec came up behind me with a chair. Furious with myself, and fighting for control, I blinked back the tears and took Paul's hand, finding calming phrases. I wanted to be able to say, 'You'll soon be better. We'll take you home and everything will be fine again.' But how could it be? Nothing had been 'fine' for years.

Somehow I stayed calm for half an hour while I talked to him, calm as I went to find Pips and left Alec to have a few minutes with him, calm as the charge nurse said this sedation would have to last another week. Then in the car, as we turned out onto the main road to go home, the dam burst, and I sobbed and sobbed. Alec stopped the car after a while, but there was nothing he could say, really. He was looking nearly as grey as Paul had done. There was nothing to be gained by sitting in a still car, so I pulled myself together so that he would start the car again. By the time we got home I had devised a plan that would help me to feel that I had done something, at least. The next day I bought seven bars of Paul's favourite chocolate, one for each day he would be restrained, wrapped them up individually, and put a little letter in with each bar. 'Dear Paul, Here is some chocolate for you. I hope you are feeling better today, Love, Mummy and Daddy.' In the one for the last day I wrote, 'I am sure you are much better now and will be getting up soon.' These were parcelled off with an explanatory note. I couldn't fill the great hole in Paul's life or mine, but I got quite good at papering over it.

Paul recovered as expected, and life carried on. Before long a lady who had been contacted through the Mothers' Union undertook to pop in and visit him from time to time, and the parents of another boy, who lived nearer at hand than we did, included him in on their visits, bringing him sweets. I was so grateful to these people. We could only manage the three-and-a-half hour journey once a month, because after a few hours with Paul we had to trail all the way back again.

Each visit I had to come to terms again with the restrictions of Paul's life. He was now a young teenager, who should have a fulfilling life ahead of him, and he was not being stretched in any way. How could I think of the future with any degree of hope, when the present was just a 'holding' operation, designed to maintain a peaceful state of affairs?

He may have been no trouble to the staff, but the barrenness and hopelessness of his situation lay on my heart like a lump of lead.

# CHAPTER EIGHT

Richard, meanwhile, continued at the Sheiling School and seemed happy there. His behaviour on his occasional trips home was rather unpredictable, which meant I was on edge all the time. Above all we never knew how bad the epileptic fits were going to be. Often, though, he surprised us by being very reasonable for days on end.

Alec enjoyed life a little more now. He developed a friendship with Ted, a Roman Catholic who seemed to be able to draw him out on the subject of faith. It was Ted who lent Alec a book by Cardinal Newman, which he read from cover to cover, and who invited him to watch the Pope's New Year Speech together on his television.

I was never sure whether my interest would be seen as an intrusion, so I tended to content myself with a very general, 'Did you have a good time with Ted?' and his equally vague reply didn't tell me much. I prayed constantly that Alec would turn to God, and would have been very happy if the Roman Catholic Church had met his need where my own didn't. However, nothing in the way of a breakthrough seemed to be happening, so I just kept praying.

Ted also joined us regularly on Friday evenings to listen to our classical records, many of which were of sacred music, both organ and choral, which were Alec's favourites. Altogether, the pressure seemed to be off us for the moment.

Pips too was discovering a new purpose in her life. For some months she had been playing quite complicated music on the piano by ear. I asked her how she knew what to play with the left hand, and she could only say, 'I just know.' One day she was playing 'Jesu, Joy of man's desiring'.

'How do you know that?' I asked.

'Elizabeth used to play it at the Family Holiday Week, of course,' she replied. I did a rapid calculation: that tune had been stored in her mind when she was only four!

We really couldn't afford piano lessons, because we were still paying off Paul's school debt. Still, we felt we had to do something. We found a good teacher for a trial lesson, which turned into four. These were such a promising and satisfying start that we knew we had to go on, although we made Pips promise that she would work at her music. Her progress was amazing to us, and brought into her life a whole new dimension which grew and grew in importance to her.

Because I had always had my hands so full with the boys, it had never occurred to us to have a pet. It would have been pushing Paul too far to have a dog in the house, and Alec thought there were too many cats around already. But when Pips was offered a kitten, I discovered a depth of feeling in her for animals that I hadn't suspected. Alec remained firm, and a very disappointed little Pips went off to bed.

'Is there any real reason why she can't have a kitten?' I asked Alec. 'It would make her so happy.' There was a long silence, then a sigh, then a smile.

'Oh, all right, as long as I don't have to have anything to do with it.'

Pips went off after school, skipping with joy, and came back with the sweetest fluffy black kitten. A bed was made out of a cardboard box and a little pink blanket, and Pips played so much with it that by the time Alec came back from work it was asleep, exhausted, in the corner of the kitchen. No one mentioned it.

Half way through his tea, Alec suddenly saw it.

'Oh, what a beautiful little kitten,' he crooned, completely won over. Pips and I grinned at each other. Guess who made the greatest fuss of little Peterkins!

Richard was now over the age range of his current school, and to our amazement they just sent him home. We had no idea of when he would be able to move on to the older boys' unit of the Rudolf Steiner School at Thornbury.

Rather despondent, we tried to find jobs to occupy him at home, but it wasn't easy. The epileptic fits I could understand, and could in no way blame him for. What I couldn't cope with were the sudden episodes of violence, screaming, roaring and shouting, often damaging valuable things which got in the way. My favourite pictures and the glass in the grandfather clock were some of the casualties. I felt that somehow he should have been able to control himself better, but he was so big and threatening at these times that I felt quite helpless. Then often he would have a prolonged fit soon afterwards, and I would feel that I hadn't been fair in my assessment. There was probably some relationship between the violence and the fits, and I should no more expect him to control one than the other.

Over this period of having Richard at home, the washing machine, the boiler and the record player all went wrong in quick succession, and Alec's grim cheerfulness — at full stretch already because his father's health was worrying him — deserted him. Suddenly one day, when

Richard was playing up, he broke down and cried uncontrollably. The doctor gave him a sedative, and I longed to pray with him. Yet I knew that for Alec it just made everything worse to think about God. If God could do all these terrible things, then he either wasn't a strong God or he wasn't a loving God. When I stood back and tried to be rational about our situation, I had problems squaring that question up myself. But beyond that, in my life there was a habit, a necessity of asking God for strength in every situation, and he always answered in one way or another.

At this sticky time, a holiday came to our aid. Paul stayed at the hospital, and after a couple of weeks camping in Tenby and Aberystwyth, and visiting Caldy Island and some glorious countryside and Richard behaving quite reasonably, we felt refreshed in body and mind. Without a holiday each year, I simply would not have coped. We always felt a need to get away to wild places, and I saw the holidays as God's provision for my psychological needs. Between the anticipation, the enjoyment of the actual holiday and the memory of it afterwards, I milked out every possible benefit and thanked God for these breaks. This particular holiday was made even better by good news when we returned – there was a space for Richard at the Steiner School for older boys. He soon settled in there happily.

The charge nurse of Paul's hospital unit suggested that we should have Paul home for a few days, and we decided to risk it. His first visit went very well. On Sunday I took him down to church, and also took him into the empty church one weekday and said a prayer with him. He liked this; it seemed to reach him in a way that nothing else could.

On his second visit home, however, he and I crossed each other's paths on the stairs one morning and suddenly his hands were round my throat, gripping me tight. I thought he was going to strangle me, and prayed an arrow prayer for instant help while scrabbling at his hands. Just as suddenly he let me go, and I collapsed onto the stairs. We both sat there, me breathing heavily, and he too seemed to go limp. After a while I said quietly, 'Would you like to help me water the garden, Paul?' and he agreed. Soon he was busily doing this as though nothing had happened. While I thanked God for this outcome, I felt strongly that Satan had his finger in this somewhere, determined to undermine any progress Paul made. I prayed against any influence of this kind, but when Alec came back I was still in shock and we decided that we would have to take Paul back to his hospital unit.

We took a picnic and told Paul we were going for a drive, but he soon realised where we were going, and shouted, 'Not go back to hospital!' When I said we had to, he went for me again, biting my arm. Alec immediately turned the car round and went back to a Police Station we had just passed. Unperturbed by my fear of the reception we would get, he explained that his autistic son had attacked his wife in the car, and he was disabled, and could we have someone to control Paul until we could get to a doctor.

The police were very understanding, and sent a Cadet in the back of the car with Paul to the local hospital where they had alerted a doctor who stood by with a syringe. Where my pride would have struggled on, Alec knew when to pull out all the stops! In twenty minutes Paul was asleep, and Alec drove as fast as he dared to get him as near his hospital unit as we could before he woke up. The sedation only lasted two hours, but when he woke I said calmly, 'Shall we have our sandwiches now?' and Alec found a good place to pull off the road. Paul was alert and happy, and after a couple of sandwiches he looked up and said, 'Going back to hospital now?'

'Yes, Paul, that's right,' I said, as nonchalantly as I could, praying hard. He just nodded and went on eating. My eyes crossed with Alec's in relief, and my heart reached out to God to thank him for answering my prayers again. Yet once Paul was safely returned, I realised afresh what a setback this had been, and wondered if he would ever be allowed home again.

Even worse, over the following months there were several upsets in the unit involving Paul, including a boy being tipped out of bed in the middle of the night, as well as throwing things at other boys. It was made clear to me that this could not continue, and that Paul might be transferred to the psychiatric ward of the main hospital.

With this hanging over us, and a very cold winter bringing a series of persistent coughs and colds, we all felt very tense and drained. Our curate, Roger Atkins, came round on several occasions to give us a chance to spill it all out, and Alec appreciated this a great deal. More important to me, perhaps, was a suggestion from his wife, Diana, that we should spend an evening a week talking and doing our mending together. This meant so much to me, to have someone to discuss spiritual things with. Even when she could say nothing new, and do nothing to help the practicalities of the situation, she was still there. Her friendship was all I wanted from her.

Alec's stepmother, who had always been so supportive, suddenly stepped in with the offer of a motor caravan. We were delighted even if this meant another loan, because our car was really not up to much: we regularly had quite long distances to travel, and holidays would be so much cheaper. When she made it clear that this was to be a gift, we were absolutely amazed.

I must admit that our first trip in the new Dormobile was not a huge success. I was terribly worried about Paul, as we had been told that our fears had now been realised: because of 'disturbed behaviour' he was now in a locked ward. I dreaded finding out what further restriction this entailed.

We had arranged to visit Richard at his new school in Thornbury and go on to see Paul in his hospital unit.

Richard's school allowed us to park our Dormobile in the farmyard attached to the school. It was very cold, but after all it wasn't like sleeping in a tent, was it? We had a hot meal, and tucked ourselves up with sleeping bags, extra blankets and hot water bottles — but I still shivered all night. In the morning there was white frost actually inside the van, so perhaps it wasn't a fair test. Someone came out and invited us to breakfast in the school kitchen, where we thawed out by the Aga cooker. Then we resumed our journey to Paul.

Actually seeing Paul the next morning was even worse than I had been able to imagine in that long cold night. He was locked in a ward of schizophrenic men, the only youngster at thirteen years old. Not only was no training provided, he wasn't even allowed out by himself in the grounds. The staff did what they could for him, allowing him to arrange his toys and other belongings as he wanted to in his room. He seemed happy, but I couldn't accept this fate for him.

'You must be able to see that this is all wrong!' I stormed at the doctor in a side office.

'Are you saying that he is being badly treated?' he replied.

'Well no, of course not. It's not that.' I tried to organise the storm of my emotions so I could sound reasonable, closing my eyes for a moment and taking a deep breath.

'Look, all the others are at least twice his age. What is he supposed to do all day?'

'Well, there is the television, and one of the nurses will take him out for a walk when the work-load on the ward permits.'

'Yes, but there's no training of any sort. Surely he shouldn't be on this ward at all?'

'Mrs Menniss, your son's behaviour is very unpredictable. He needs to be under this level of surveillance. I'm sorry that it has proved a shock to you, but I agree with the consultant's decision. Paul is in the right place here.'

71

I tried another tack.

'Is there any reason why it has to be so far from home? In this sort of weather the journey is all but impossible. We used to be a close family...' I tailed off, overwhelmed by the impossibility of explaining that this 'violent patient' was, despite everything, still my son.

'Well now, if you wanted to get him transferred, your best course of action would be to take him home now and contact your local authority. Under those circumstances I think you would find they would be forced to find him a placement nearer home.' The doctor sounded pleased to have a positive suggestion to make, so I gave it a moment's thought. But only a moment. Cope with Paul in a violent state? Subject Pips – and myself – to more fear and danger?

'I can't see how that would be possible,' I admitted, and the interview appeared to be at an end.

At home once more, feeling desperate, I couldn't face anybody. Then I remembered Roger, our curate, who had said I could come round any time and talk. I was going on a retreat with a group led by him that weekend. Perhaps it could wait. He must be busy. For a few hours, I did nothing. I was just numb. Then suddenly, before I realised that I had decided, I was putting on my coat.

As soon as Roger opened the door, he saw the state I was in. 'Una, whatever is the matter?' he cried. 'Let me have your coat. Come into the study. Diana, put the kettle on, Una's come.' His kindness wiped out my fear of disturbing him. As calmly as I could I told him the facts, taking deep breaths and trying to meet his understanding eyes. When my threadbare account was finished, he left a few moments silence. Then quietly he said, 'Una, how does all this make you feel?' It was just the trigger I needed. Out it all came, the frustrated love, the anger at the authorities, the hopelessness, the pain of seeing Paul slip further and further away from me. I cried myself out. Then Roger knelt beside me on the floor, and prayed, 'O

God, you know how oppressed we are....' I hardly heard the rest. How oppressed *we* are. I knew now that Roger was entering into my suffering, and by the time he had finished praying, I was reassured that Christ was too.

The weekend retreat encouraged me to do something I had felt wary of before. Alone in my room, I prayed that God would lead me to a passage in the Bible which was a message for me. Trembling, I opened my Bible in John's Gospel at the account of the raising of Lazarus from the dead. Puzzled, I wondered what this could have to say to me. When I reached verse 40 of chapter 11, it was as if the words Jesus spoke to Martha rang in my own ears: I read them over and over, marvelling.

'Did I not tell you that if you believed, you would see the glory of God?'

From that moment I knew that I had to go on believing that God would be glorified in Paul's life – and one day it would happen.

# CHAPTER NINE

For the next few months it was Richard's placement that caused us the most concern. The Rudolf Steiner School just couldn't cope with him any longer, and, since he was nearly sixteen, he would have had to leave fairly soon anyway. I felt he had been treated there with a great deal of understanding of his problems, and that for him it had been an environment which had stretched and educated him as well as possible. Even this decision to remove him, which seemed to go against us, was because of the welfare of the other boys. I remain very grateful for the time these schools were available to both boys.

So Richard, despite being 'unmanageable', was at home with no future planned. Now we would find out for ourselves what the school meant by that label.

Our first trip out was to Audrey's caravan in the woods, a lovely spot in April. We went out by bus, with Pips who was still on school holiday. Despite the peace which was wonderful as we rambled among the spring flowers, Richard had several fits, and in the end I had to go in search of a telephone to get a message to Alec. He came to find us after work, had tea with us, and drove us home. I couldn't face the bus and then the walk with the possibility of a fit at any moment.

To my amazement and delight, three days after Richard's sixteenth birthday, we actually had a visit from a Mental Welfare Officer, arranging for him to attend Fareham Adult Training Centre, with transport provided. This was the first time in years that the authorities had done anything for Richard that had not been prompted by a crisis. I couldn't foresee what this would do for him, but it looked like a real breakthrough, and in the interval before he could begin there I prayed hard that it would work out. I really wanted him to be able to live at home, however much it cost me in effort, but for his sake he needed to have a life of his own, and I couldn't have coped without a little break every day. This looked ideal.

I began to have my doubts, however, when the tantrums started. A squabble over the television with Pips was the blue touch paper for the first incident; two days later the bus we were waiting for didn't turn up, and he made a really violent scene in the street, kicking, screaming and throwing himself around. I was terrified someone would get hurt, and so apparently was a passer-by, who fetched a policeman. In the presence of this stern, burly and official-looking man, Richard calmed down and walked home. Three cups of tea later, I had calmed down as well, but I was left exhausted. Did I really want him living at home?

I was out baby-sitting and so missed the next incident: Richard went for Pips in a very malicious way, terrifying Alec. What a quandary for him, alone. He didn't want them in the same room together, and he needed to get help, but which one was he to leave alone? His on-the-spot decision was to bundle Pips into the van, get her to the police station, explain, rush back to Richard, and leave the police to follow with Pips. He got back dreading the thought that Richard might have been tearing the house apart, but in fact everything was under control when I came home an hour later. Now it was Alec's turn to receive the ministry of the tea-pot!

In the week before Richard was due to start at the centre, his fits doubled in number, and the doctor prescribed more phenobarbitone. This certainly seemed to pay off, as he enjoyed his first week very much, and a note from the instructor suggested that he would settle.

That year we took him on holiday with us to Wales, camping in the new Dormobile. This wasn't very relaxing when his behaviour was so unpredictable, but we managed. Then, two days after we got back, he was returned in the middle of the day from the Training Centre. They said he had 'gone berserk' and that they couldn't have him again.

I couldn't blame them for their decision, but it threw the weight back on me again, and this time, instead of being flattered, I felt indignant that I should be asked to cope with the unmanageable by myself. I changed the focus of my prayers from 'Help him to stay at home' to 'Help us find another placement for him – quickly!'

God knew I couldn't take any more at this stage, and provided a place at Oldthorpe Hospital, only eleven miles from home. There was to be some delay, but a few days later Richard terrorised everyone in the local Post Office by screaming and kicking at anyone who came near him. After two hours of this, during which they somehow got him to the police station, he went from there straight to Oldthorpe under a 'temporary order' signed by a doctor, with my grateful consent. It was hardly an auspicious start at the place where he was to spend the next ten years!

Having seen how well Richard settled, we began a campaign for Paul to be transferred there, and after five months of promises, hope, and sometimes feeling it would never happen, we won. Both boys under the same roof, to be visited together, and only eleven miles away. This was wonderful! Paul hadn't been home for well over a year at this point, and we really didn't feel in touch with him at all. Now he was within reach.

Our first visit soon dashed our optimism, however. Far from being in Richard's villa, or another similar one, we discovered Paul was in a locked unit, with patients far more severely handicapped than himself. We tackled the most senior member of staff we could find, who patiently gave us an explanation.

'Well, Paul is far more prone to fits of violence than Richard, according to the notes which came with him, so he must be in a villa where we have a high staff-patient ratio. It's for his own good, you know.'

We had heard it before, and were soon to hear it again. We got the name of the person ultimately in charge, and wrote to him, but he took very much the same line. I had to admit I didn't really know what Paul's behaviour had been like recently, and hoped that in time they would be proved wrong so he could live under the same régime as Richard.

The contrast was painful. Richard had people to play with, some educational input, could go out for walks, and even to church occasionally. Paul, with those of his fellow-inmates who could get around, had the 'freedom' of a patch of grass at the back of the unit surrounded by high-wire netting. He had no occupational therapy at all. There were no books, no one of his own age to talk to, nothing but television and the inside of the same room, day in, day out. We immediately began to contest this through every means open to us, but nothing happened. Then we discovered a new problem.

For three or four consecutive visits we were told, 'Paul doesn't want to come out today.' Certainly he looked very apathetic and listless, and often dirty and untidy as well. One week I asked if I couldn't just take him round to Richard's villa so they could spend some time together, which didn't seem to happen unless I was there.

'Oh,' tutted the nurse, annoyed, 'in that case I'll have to find some other clothes and clean him up a bit.'

'Just get me his clothes,' I said through clenched teeth. 'I'll save you the bother.' The next time we arrived, he was spick and span, and we had a lovely walk together. After that, I trusted the staff when they said he was too disturbed. We heard no more of Paul not wanting to come out.

From time to time our letters roused the authorities to the point of granting us an interview, but we always seemed to get someone different. Some were embarrassed by my questions, some didn't seem to realise that the needs of autistic patients were quite different from those of the severely mentally handicapped. The best breaks came when I spoke to someone who admitted they didn't know the rationale for what was going on, and had enough conscience to do something. One doctor arranged for Paul to go to a gym three times a week, but it was only a couple of months before the instructor was 'no longer available'.

At least for the first couple of years we could sometimes bring Paul home to tea, although never to stay overnight. Then one day he suddenly lashed out in the Dormobile, kicking through a cupboard door, and we realised again just how vulnerable we were if anything went wrong. Yet how could I withdraw from the only way I felt I was doing any good?

A recent test had proclaimed that 'due to mental illness Paul is functioning intellectually at a very low level'. I was livid about this, not only because this report wasn't shown to us until the hospital had had it for two months, but because I couldn't see how they could expect Paul to 'develop intellectually' if they treated him like a cabbage. The hospital obviously worked on the principle that he should be kept out of sight and out of mind, but there was no way I could do the same. Whatever he was, he was my son. As long as we could, we had to keep bringing him home.

At last a solution presented itself: we would have to take someone else with us, strong enough to be a buffer between Paul and Alec when he was driving, and to hold Paul down if required. Once again we were dependent on friends. Yet even this didn't always make it possible for Paul to come home.

When he was showing 'disturbed behaviour', he was sedated and isolated in a cell-like room with no outside view. There was only an opaque glass window high up in the wall and a very small reinforced glass panel in the door which lead to the main ward. To let us in, the nurse unlocked the door from the ward, ushered us into a narrow passage, squeezed back past us to lock the door again, then went to unlock the door to Paul's cell. I stared, numb. Is this where he had been every time we had heard 'Paul is too disturbed to see you today'? All these precautions might be necessary for some patients, but my Paul? In the cell was nothing but his bed: no books, nothing to look at. On one occasion the charge nurse complained that he had torn up his bed-linen.

'Just what else is he supposed to do?' I replied, and got a funny look.

The picture that always came to me when I agonised over Paul's situation was that he was like a plant confined to a dark cellar, and he could never grow strong and healthy without the sunlight of more mental stimulation. I felt strongly that, given the opportunity, he would improve mentally, he could be transferred to somewhere more stimulating, and we would be on an upward spiral. As it was, we were consistently blocked on the first step. He was now sixteen, and had had no education for six years.

One worry at the back of our minds was, 'What will happen to the boys when we are gone?' About this time we heard of the Trusteeship Scheme of the National Society for the Mentally Handicapped. This provided, in the case of the death of either parent, a visitor once a month and for birthdays. They would satisfy themselves that all was well with the child, would talk to the hospital if they were concerned about anything, and had the back-up of the society if needed. This sounded perfect, and would give us a lot of peace of mind, but we needed to take out insurance to cover the cost, which we could do only if I worked part-time to pay the premiums.

Obviously some kind of work in a school would make it possible for me to be with Pips during the holidays, so I was pleased to accept a job in the kitchens of a secondary school. When I was no longer needed there I became a playground attendant, then after a miserable term cleaning up an indescribable art room every evening, I graduated to 'lollipop lady' for a Roman Catholic school just down the road. This I did for many years in all weathers, and made lots of little friends as we waited together by the roadside. On several occasions I was brutally reminded why I was there, as maniacal drivers screeched to a halt within inches of me. Later at home I would still be trembling from fear and rage.

Apart from the job, I found time during these years of a fairly settled state of affairs for several interests and concerns. I had enjoyed French at school for nine years, but along with everything else not connected to survival, this had been forgotten. Now I made contact with Thérèse, a lady who had married an Englishman and lived nearby, and we soon became firm friends. My French was never more than adequate, but it got us through a holiday in France, and helped me to feel I had some life of my own.

With regular church attendance, which was something I would never take for granted again, I could expand my horizons in this direction too. The ecumenical movement had interested me for some time, and I organised several coffee mornings, with discussion, for friends who between them represented the Anglican, Roman Catholic, Congregational, Methodist and Baptist

81

churches, and the Salvation Army.

In time, these monthly gatherings attracted the attention of the BBC. In spite of the crush, which was bad enough normally in my small living room, we squeezed in an interviewer, a large camera and two cameramen as well! It was good to be involved in something where there could be an exchange of ideas, although I have to say I was more impressed by the amount we had in common than by any differences which arose. On a practical level we were already united, and theological differences often seemed irrelevant.

Although I was eager to put behind me those years when I had been obsessed with the boys, they were both still very much a part of every day. When I was apart from them, I often used to feel that no one else really understood what a burden I carried. So it was that I put an advertisement in the local paper to enquire whether there were any parents of autistic children who would value meeting for mutual support.

My motives may have been purely selfish to begin with, but I soon found myself on the committee of a newly-formed 'Hampshire Autistic Society'. This existed not only for the support of parents, but to organise outings and holidays for the children, and to raise funds. The nervous energy expended for an outing was always terrific, but it was worth it to be in a group situation where you didn't have constantly to apologise, explain, and feel guilty. Of course, it was quite a problem finding venues that could cope with such an unpredictable group. Our church had a hall which had been used for a teenage club, equipped with very second-hand sturdy furniture which was ideal. One Saturday a month we descended with picnic teas and ran riot – it was wonderful. Paul always loved these gatherings, and I did my best to get him to as many as possible.

Another side of the Society's work was to convince the Education Authorities that autistic children needed to be catered for with specialised educational facilities. Our Chairman and I sought interviews with anyone who might be persuaded to support us in this, and soon concluded that the 'powers that be' were not going to be behind us. We then resolved that we should found a school for autistic children ourselves. In this great cause I was even prepared to overcome my quiet nature and give talks to any group who would invite me. Autism was very misunderstood, and this ignorance lay behind many of the problems we faced. After two frantic years of fund-raising, a special school, named Hope Lodge, was opened in Southampton. Paul was already beyond the age range catered for by the school, but it was good to help others by giving them the opportunities we hadn't had.

Alec supported me in this, but soon felt he had heard all too much about it, and confided to his diary on one occasion, 'Can get very little interest in anything but autistics from Una, so I keep my peace.'

Alec's own life, meanwhile, continued to revolve around the constant house improvements. He was always finding another project, usually straining himself with heavy loads, in the ongoing quest for the perfect house. It worried me that he slogged on, despite much pain and illness, but his life seemed to have no meaning for him apart from this. He hated Christmas because he was at home but couldn't 'get on'. Sitting around eating and being sociable was definitely second best. The garden was firmly left to me, which suited me fine.

Pips was doing well at school, but it was music that became the centre of her life. After a few years of piano she branched out into the trumpet and organ, with bell-ringing for relaxation. Only by great diligence was she able to fit all this in, but the concerts we attended to listen to her made it clear to us that she was making her mark. Finally after A-levels she was offered a place at the Royal School of Music. And I had been anxious about the price of piano lessons!

All this provided a welcome counterpoint to the constant worry about the boys, and Paul in particular. It was so dreadful to me, loving them both equally, to see Paul treated in such an inhuman manner. Keeping in touch was my constant aim: if they knew they were loved by someone, perhaps their lives would have some point whatever happened. We visited as often as we could, sent postcards when we were on holiday, and brought them home frequently, although Paul could never stay the night. As it was, I prayed non-stop when we had Paul out with us, especially in the car. Even Richard's visits home caused tension, because I did the absolute minimum of housework while he was with us, spending all my time and energy on enriching his life: this was something Alec could never understand, and the resentment seemed to build up between us. On most issues, however, we managed to make the strain of our situation work for us, overcoming it together, rather than letting it pull us apart.

For example, I used to get very upset if Richard was ever handed over to us with bruising on his arms or face. This didn't happen very often, but I wasn't satisfied with the explanations such as, 'He put up quite a fight yesterday.' Alec thought that was quite adequate, and we could have been fighting each other over whether to complain further. Instead, we sat down to talk about it that evening, and Alec pointed out that we often had to hold his arms very firmly behind his back, or sit on him, and it wasn't always possible to hold him even then, and we needed help. Any more force than we used, which is what was needed, probably would cause bruising.

I was further reassured when Alec continued, with a grin, 'Anyway, I've seen a few bruises on the staff as well. I really think they do a tremendous job.'

# CHAPTER TEN

Sometimes the way the administration handled Paul, and us as a family, was simply lacking in imagination. Perhaps most of the other inmates' families had taken the only realistic course of action, which was to resign themselves to the idea that their son, brother or whatever, would always be like they were then. I couldn't resign myself to this, because I believed God was saying something different. I didn't enjoy making a fuss, but felt I had to, for Paul's sake.

Often, the staff simply failed to take me into account. It was administratively necessary, for example, to get me to sign a form giving permission for some dental work. Did they expect me to sign the form and forget it? Not me! I prayed right through the time of the appointment, and phoned afterwards to make sure that everything had gone according to plan. Yes, I was assured, everything was fine.

What it was not administratively necessary to tell me was what 'treatment' had actually been given. The next visit, there was Paul, absolutely toothless. They had taken out every one. Presumably there had been quite a lot of decay, and this was the easy way out. After a while I asked about the possibility of dentures, but they didn't think Paul would cope with these, and I'm sure that was right. So Paul was doomed to toothlessness.

True, this didn't worry him at all, and eating was never a problem, but it contributed to the appearance of one who is never going to have to be in society again. Despite all medical prognostications, I believed Paul was going to reveal the glory of God, and in my mind that would involve a wider circle than a single psychiatric ward.

Actually I could understand, and therefore cope with, others' lack of expectation for Paul. The hardest thing for me was to be forced to consider that they might be right. Too much of the evidence suggested that they were.

For a period of about eighteen months there was no trouble about taking Paul out, but then we began to hear, 'I'm afraid Paul is rather too disturbed today. You can see him in his room for a few minutes if you like.' This always made me so sad, because he was missing out on a treat Richard was getting. Once, suspecting that the staff were falling into an automatic pattern, I pleaded with them. They said it was out of the question this time, but the next time they seemed prepared to let him go.

Happily we went off with both boys in the van towards a nearby forest for a walk. After a while I handed Richard a sweet, then Paul. Utterly without warning, he grabbed my hand, and forced my thumb back. My cry of 'No, Paul, no!' had Alec jamming on the brakes and rushing round to the back, but Paul had already rammed his head hard against my face and pulled out a handful of hair before Alec could reach him.

Somehow we pulled him out of the van, and a passing motorist helped us to pin him down in a ditch, sitting on his chest and legs. His eyes were completely wild, and my feelings were in turmoil. Part of me was thinking, 'Is he possessed by the devil?' and the other half was pleading with God, 'Please don't let this be the end of taking him

86

out, I can't bear it!'

Another motorist phoned for an ambulance from the nearest phone box, but it was twenty minutes before it arrived, and Paul was still thrashing around. Our combined strength was all but giving out. Two ladies from the first car sat with Richard and gave him more sweets, and there was no sign that he knew what was going on at all. When the ambulance arrived, the men walked up to Paul holding a straitjacket. Immediately he stopped writhing, and they said we should all get up.

'Now then,' said the heavier of the two ambulance men in a stern voice, 'are you going to get in our van quietly, or do we have to put you in this?' Paul's voice came meekly, 'Go quietly,' and he got up and walked over to the ambulance. I didn't know whether he had seen a straitjacket before, but he obviously saw it as a threat.

Trembling, I tried to come to grips with what needed to be done. Alec thanked the people who had so kindly helped us out, while I explained to Richard that Paul was ill and that we had to go back. He took this quite calmly, so we decided that I would go in the ambulance with Paul, and Alec would follow with Richard. I think we both just did what was needed like robots, but as soon as we were alone together again, the trembling took over. We sat together in the Dormobile in the car park, not speaking because there was nothing to say, not touching each other because Alec knew that would open the floodgates, each of us in our own private hell. Then we drove home.

What was it that made me able to go on loving Paul? He never responded to affection, or showed that he appreciated what I did for him. If to love someone means storing up emotional instalments like a bank account, in the knowledge that it will be there whenever you want it, this was quite untrue of me with Paul. I had learned through the years that I could expect no return of my love. I had to be quite selfless, and I'm no different from anyone else. I just couldn't have done it, except in God's strength. To go on loving him was to take a tremendous risk, and it would have been so easy to give up. Especially now. Love was nothing to do with my emotions any more. At this point love was reduced to bare faith in God.

I slept well, but the next morning I felt dreadful, and must have looked it as well. A new window-cleaner came round, and when I turned to find my purse I nearly fell over. He grabbed my elbow, and then saw the bruises on my face.

'Steady on,' he said kindly. 'Are you all right?'

'Yes, thank you,' I began, but the tears were already sliding down my cheeks. Before I knew what I was doing, I had poured out the whole story. How loving Paul was like trying to hug a bottomless pit. How I had to be optimistic to keep going, but how this made the disappointments all the more crushing. How this really was the end, and we would never, never, be able to take him out again....

'Just a minute,' broke in my window-cleaning friend, who I had discovered was called Alan, 'all you need is someone to be there to hold him down if he cuts up rough, right?'

'Well, yes...' I faltered. 'But who would risk being attacked like I was? Alec has to drive, and you can see what Paul can do to me....'

'I'm not talking about you and your husband holding him,' Alan said. 'How about me? I'm a boxer. I reckon I could deal with your young man.' I gave him a quick look over, and decided he was right.

'But why should you?' I was non-plussed.

'Cos I want to.' End of argument.

What I couldn't go into was the fact that there had been no violence for so long that I felt Paul was improving. I thought that to go without an escort showed faith. Now suddenly this explosion of violence against myself rocked me completely. Nothing Alan did could take that sting away, but he did make it possible for us to take Paul out again, and I was so grateful to him for that. Above all, he showed that he cared.

On our first trip we just went for a short walk with Paul, but Alan's confidence was such that he brought his wife and three-year-old son with him. Everything went well, and this began several months of a weekly commitment for Alan, for which I could never thank him enough.

Once I had come to realise that a strong man made all the difference to the feasibility of these trips the church stepped in. Alan Harrison, our new vicar, took the lead in this, coming with me as often as he could, and detailing off his curate for this unaccustomed duty when he couldn't. With this example to follow, many church members offered their services as well. It would have been very difficult for me to ask anyone personally, but to have it organised on my behalf was bliss.

Paul and I were not the only ones to benefit from this rota system. Once people had got involved to that extent, they often showed enough interest to help with an Autistics Outing or something similar. Our church was certainly being made aware of the various forms of handicaps, and many of our helpers expressed their surprise that these 'problem children' could be so much fun. It helped them to think about the purpose of life, and the love of God, in quite a different way.

One busy father obviously had given this some thought, and spelled it out for me one day as we drove back from returning the boys to their wards.

'You take Richard and Paul for example. They're obviously never going to hold down jobs, or have a family, or do many of the things which occupy most people most of the time. But does this mean there's no purpose in their life? Who says that's what life is all about, anyway? Jesus himself wouldn't score very high if that was what counted. So the purpose of life must be something deeper. And what I ask myself is, "Am I so busy doing things which are not ultimately important that I haven't got time for the things that are?"'

'Wouldn't you say that showing love comes pretty high up the list?' I reassured him, 'because that's just what you're doing by giving us your time and coming out with us today.'

Alec had reacted to this 'religious conversation' by concentrating on the road, but he gave a nod and a grunt of assent at this point. The support and encouragement of the church had given him something to think about as well.

'Well, you might be right there,' answered our helper, 'but I wouldn't have seen it that way unless I had come, and I had to come before I really understood why. It's a sort of vicious circle of not understanding. How can you get people to break out of it?'

'Well, that doesn't seem to be a problem in our church,' I laughed. 'Perhaps people just see that God loves them, God loves Paul, so they must show love to Paul, and they sign up.'

'Or perhaps they are shamed into giving it a go because if the vicar, busy as he is, can give it priority, they ought to as well!'

Certainly Alan Harrison had been a wonderful support. On our first visit he had played and walked with the boys and showed great sensitivity to their problems. On the way home we had visited Romsey Abbey where Alan had prayed with and for both boys. This was such an encouragement to my own prayers. So rarely could I pray openly for the boys while I was with them, because of Alec, and if he weren't there, I would have been unsure of their reaction if I laid hands on them. For some reason, the boys were happy to allow Alan that authority, and I was so strengthened by this memory in the weeks ahead.

Because I felt Alan really cared about my situation, it was him I turned to when Paul went through another patch of not being allowed out. I was so convinced that it was because of lack of mental stimulation. Alan said he would arrange to come with me to tackle the authorities, and made an appointment for us two days later with the Medical Superintendent. When we arrived we were told he was not available, but we could see another doctor. Of course we did this, but it wasn't very satisfactory because

90

she didn't know Paul and could only say that she would pass our message on. We were restrained in our comments in front of her – after all, it wasn't her fault – but in the car, Alan let out his real thoughts.

'Una, you shouldn't take any more of this. It's disgusting.'

'I know,' I answered grimly, 'but what can I do? This is what always happens.'

'Well, it's not good enough. The sooner you get Paul out of here the better.'

'But where could he go? His reports will go with him, he'll be treated in the same way, and he'll be further away from home. I can't see any way forward.'

'I'm not surprised, if you've been fighting on your own all this time. What you need is a bit of back-up.'

A couple of months later I collected Paul for a walk, but was very on edge about him, because he kept starting out on walks, but then coming back to the van again. Then I noticed that he was walking awkwardly and took off his shoes. They were at least a size too small, and his feet were covered with sores. I reported this to a nurse when we got back, and he promised that this would never happen again. Nothing he said could really stop my unease from mounting. The next visit, Paul was again 'disturbed'. The years were passing, and did I really have to accept that Paul would never know any other kind of life?

On one of Paul's birthdays I took some crayons and a colouring book, and afterwards was taken on one side by the charge nurse.

'It doesn't matter this time,' he said, 'but you really should ask permission before doing that again. It counts as occupational therapy you see, and you're not a member of the union.'

These things eventually became a tremendous burden that I carried night and day, and which threatened to break me. Then suddenly one night I cried out, 'Oh God, you take over.'

Immediately there came into my mind the name of a

91

doctor who I had heard some time ago give a lecture for the Mentally Handicapped Society. As I spoke to him afterwards he had discovered that he lived quite near me, so he had offered to take me home. He had been so sympathetic, but at the time it hadn't seemed important that he worked for the Regional Hospital Board. Now suddenly the two facts, long forgotten, came back to my mind and fitted together. I knew this had to be God working through my memory.

I sat down immediately and wrote a long letter to him, telling of my many anxieties about Paul and his enforced idleness for the eight years he had now been at Oldthorpe. I told him of my appeals to the hospital to provide occupation for Paul, all of which had fallen on deaf ears.

By return of post came a letter asking if he could make an immediate appointment to see me.

'I'll make no bones about it, Mrs Menniss,' he began once I had shown him to a chair, 'I was shocked by your letter. Shocked, and very distressed. I showed it to the Senior Administrative Officer of the Board, who reacted in quite the same way.' We talked for a while, as I expanded my thoughts, and finally agreed on a course of action.

'You re-write the letter you wrote to me,' he summarised, 'but address it to the Senior Administrative Officer, and you have my word that some action will be taken.' That man didn't know how narrowly he escaped being hugged. This was the first ray of hope for years. Instead I had to wait until he had gone and 'hug' God with my praise!

First came an acknowledgement of my letter, then the information that the situation at Oldthorpe was being investigated, then that there was to be a meeting to decide on a course of action. Within two months of my letter, I had a visit from two representatives of the Regional Board.

'We've been into the conditions of all the patients at Oldthorpe with regard to occupation,' they said, 'and have discovered that not only Paul and all of his villa, but others as well, would benefit from having something to do. It has been agreed to build a Special Training Unit, with a high staff/patient ratio, for these patients.'

'That's wonderful,' I enthused, 'but how long is it going to take?'

'At least a year,' they admitted, 'but we've already been allocated the funds to cover the salaries of the occupational therapists, so we are recruiting them now, and they will just work with small groups in the villas for the moment.'

'But I suggested that to the hospital years ago,' I said, puzzled. 'Why is it suddenly possible now?'

'It looks as though your letters weren't reaching anybody who had the power or the concern to do anything, Mrs Menniss. There have been some changes in the administration, and I think you'll find everything quite different now.'

I did indeed find a new responsiveness. Not long after this, Paul started to lose weight visibly: the staff said about eleven pounds in a month. They were concerned, but said he was eating normally. They put him on a high protein diet, and he began to gain again. Two visits later, I heard he was being treated for anaemia, and eventually he stabilised at about five pounds less than his original weight. No cause for any of this was ever established, but even while I was still worried, I was reassured that I would be kept informed and that something was being done.

When the occupational therapy materialised, the staff reported that Paul was very co-operative, and on the whole his behaviour improved. I felt that this justified my attitude, and was impatient for the day when he could not only have more time doing something constructive, but get out of the villa for a while as well. Richard was so happy in his villa, it was difficult to believe they were under the same administration.

Finally, a staff nurse nervously took me on one side when I arrived for a visit.

'I thought you would like to know, Mrs Menniss, that the Special Unit for Occupational Therapy opened last week.'

'That's wonderful,' I enthused. 'They've only taken just over a year, like they said.'

'Yes, indeed,' he murmured. 'But I'm afraid there's some bad news as well.'

'Yes?' I was instantly subdued, but ready.

'Paul is not eligible to attend.'

That was the one thing I wasn't ready for. I must have stood there with my mouth open, for the nurse continued.

'We have tried to give Paul odd jobs around the villa, because of course all the occupational therapists are now over at the Unit. I played football with him yesterday in the enclosure, but we can't do anything educational—only the occupational therapists are allowed to do that. The best we can do isn't good enough.'

'Then I shall have to fight again.' I had recovered my balance by now, and looked him firmly in the eye. 'Thank you for your concern, and for telling me.'

That night my frustration and anger at the authorities just boiled over. I was bewildered. I was livid. I stormed, first at Alec then, when he could take no more, at God. But it wasn't them I was angry with so I sat down to write a letter to the hospital board, expressing myself fairly forcefully.

After some explanation of the different categories of patient they felt they could cope with, and some reasons why Paul wasn't in such a category, they decided to 'bend the rules' and let him go for a trial period. Perhaps they sensed that I was ready to bend heads if they didn't!

Of course I couldn't be sure that Paul would toe the line, and I prayed solidly through his first three sessions. There were four therapists, and they took twelve patients at a time. Under this régime, Paul not only behaved, but produced some simple craft work and painting.

When, with great pride, he showed it to me, I cried.

# CHAPTER ELEVEN

This added stimulation didn't put an end to Paul's problems, needless to say. His behaviour remained 'unpredictable', which was the only way I could let myself describe the senseless violence he was capable of. He couldn't come home for Christmas, although we celebrated it again for him on Boxing Day. As we went into the next year the pattern continued of taking both boys out, but only bringing Richard home.

Alan Harrison was coming to the end of his ministry in Eastleigh, and other people from the church came with us for the outings. While I was praying one day, however, I felt very strongly that I was to ask Alan to anoint Paul before he left. He was very happy to do this, and came across with me to collect Paul and take him into a nearby church, where he anointed him for healing, and also prayed that he would be freed from any domination of Satan. This was a great comfort to me, as I had often felt that Satan had an undue influence in Paul's violent behaviour, although I knew very little about this sort of thing and would have been hard put to explain what I meant.

Richard was always very good at home, and shared my delight in wild flowers and birds, so we had many pleasant outings. I was increasingly worried by his fits, though, which seemed to be more frequent and prolonged. If they occurred in the night, we would hear strange hooting and wailing noises, and I would go and sit with him. One night he was deeply unconscious for half an hour, which was longer than I had ever known. The other problem was that he would usually wet the bed. Now the fits began to have this effect during the day, and one visit was curtailed because I ran out of clean clothes for him.

Our new vicar, John Hobbs, took us back to Oldthorpe, and was most concerned. From that point on, he declared himself ready to follow his predecessor and help out with 'Paul duty'. This didn't surprise me, because he gave the impression of being a 'gentle giant', a very tall man who just oozed love for everyone. But I hadn't taken it for granted that he would take this on with the pressures of his new appointment, and I was very grateful that he did.

The next trip was for Richard's birthday. We took both boys to Fritham woods, where the bluebells were wonderful. John was quite taken aback by Richard's knowledge of flowers. It was doing Richard good to show off a little, so I said, 'Oh look, Richard, what's that?' and pointed to a plant under a tree some way off.

'Wood spurge,' he answered proudly.

'Surely he doesn't know that!' protested John.

'Go and touch the wood spurge, Richard,' I laughed and winked at John. 'John doesn't know which one it is.' And he did. Then we had a lovely picnic with as many birthday treats as I could easily bring with me.

A fortnight later, Pips came home from college to play her trumpet in a concert, which we were all looking forward to. But at eight the next morning I had a message that shattered all our excitement. Richard had died in the night, of a fit.

No one had said that this was possible. Alec had already gone to work, so I went round to a neighbour who phoned him, and made me a cup of tea until he could get there. Alec was obviously deeply shocked as well, but his first thought was to donate Richard's eyes, because we knew he had exceptionally good sight. The hospital said we had to be there by mid-day to sign the necessary forms.

Then we went home, to wake a sleeping Pips and break the news to her. She was distraught. The morning passed in a blur: John Hobbs came, and another of our 'helpers', then we went over to Oldthorpe. Alec was determined to make Richard's eyes available for transplant. Somehow it was a symbol to him of salvaging something from the horror of it all.

That evening, Pips decided she could not let the choral society down, and Alec and I went for moral support. Alec even recorded the concert. In his diary that night Alec wrote: 'Loving Richard died. He came to teach us joy in simplicity.'

The next day, Pips was bellringing in a beautiful country church, and Alec and I sat there, glad to get away from the tumult of organisation that seemed necessary, and feeling closer to each other in our grief than we had for a long time.

The day after that was Sunday, and as I was getting ready for church, Alec suddenly said, 'I'm coming with you.'

Few of the congregation had heard of Richard's death, but the first item on the newsheet was 'The funeral of Richard Menniss will be....' I could just feel the waves of compassion being directed at us, although I found it difficult to reply to any of the things people said as we left. Alec was overwhelmed: 'I really felt loved, as though all those people really cared. I'm beginning to understand what Christianity is all about.' We went home and together we wrote the announcement to the local paper:

'Richard, handicapped son of Alec and Una Menniss, called by God to be made perfect.'

The funeral was at the crematorium the following Friday, and John Hobbs and I together planned a service which stressed that Richard was now with God. We had one of Richard's favourite hymns, 'All things bright and beautiful' and in his short address John said, 'All of us know God to a greater or lesser degree, but Richard's knowledge of God is now far greater than that of any of us.' I was deeply moved by that thought.

The service ended as we all stood to hear a recording of 'In Paradisam' from Fauré's *Requiem*. John Hobbs read to us the words in English:

'May the angels receive thee in paradise; at thy coming may the martyrs receive thee, and bring thee into the Holy City, Jerusalem. There may the choir of angels receive thee, and with Lazarus, once a beggar, may thou have eternal rest.'

There was just a simple red and white cross from the family, and a bunch of all the flowers Richard loved – red campion, bluebells, stitchwort and buttercups – which Pips had cycled round the lanes to pick.

The cross was brought back to church, where everyone could see both it and the beautiful inscription Alec had written with such care on the white card.

'In memory of our loving Richard. You enriched our lives by showing us joy in simplicity, Richard.'

We asked friends, instead of giving flowers, to give donations to the hospital's swimming pool fund, and they were most generous.

From then on, Alec came to church every week. 'It suddenly means so much more,' he explained. 'And everyone is so welcoming – I never feel as though anyone is thinking "What's he doing here?" And that new Communion Service is really very good – though I don't think I want to take Communion just yet,' he added hurriedly, anticipating my question. 'I don't know why... I'm just not ready.'

That Sunday afternoon was very painful – we went back to Oldthorpe to take Paul out. He was very smartly dressed and we went out for a walk, had a game of football and had tea in the Dormobile. My heart felt like lead, knowing we could never take Richard out again. As we returned Paul, we met a patient from Richard's villa, who announced cheerfully, 'Richard's dead. Did you know?' Paul had no idea what had happened, and even this didn't seem to get through to him. The nurses on Paul's unit were very kind, and said Paul was doing well at the Special Training Unit, but it was a very difficult day to get through.

The following day was a Bank Holiday, and thundery. Richard had always been fascinated by unusual weather, and in fact had driven us nearly mad on occasion by his running commentary during storms. Now, however, we would have done anything to be driven mad like that again.

'I feel as though Richard is signalling to us through the thunder.' Alec tried to smile at the quaintness of this idea, but failed. After dinner we sat quietly in a country church for a long time. Alec's diary expressed so much that he didn't feel he could burden me with.

*Tuesday:* Back to work after a weekend quite unlike anything I've ever known. Una met me at mid-day to have lunch in the Rec, and we looked at many messages of sympathy. In the evening we had visitors, but I felt weary at heart and went to bed.

*Thursday:* Dark clouds – Richard would have loved watching them. Received another pile of sympathy letters. Spent the evening writing, and just talking to Una. She is very brave.

I knew I had to be brave, though my heart was so heavy, because Alec kept breaking down and crying, and I felt I must find comforting words for him. His depression went on and on, and it was no help when the doctor said he was going to need a hernia operation.

The next time I saw Audrey, she told me of a dream which she'd had.

'There was a sunken garden, and in the middle there was a fountain playing. There were a number of happy young people in the garden, and someone was asleep on a bench. Suddenly he sat up, and one of the others quickly ran over to him and gave him a drink from the fountain. As he turned, I saw it was Richard, a Richard now made perfect. Then I became aware that there was music playing, and it was "Jesu, joy of man's desiring".'

'I don't know what it means,' admitted Audrey, 'but I just knew I had to tell you. I felt very comforted myself.'

'Bless you, Audrey.' I gave her a tearful hug. It was one of many little ways in which I was reassured.

Because there had been an inquest, we had to believe that there had been no neglect by the staff in his villa. The death certificate gave the cause of death as asphyxia, which seemed a terrible thing, and I couldn't help remembering the nights I had sat beside him while he was unconscious in a fit. Now there was nothing more we could do.

A month after the funeral, John Hobbs took us to the country to scatter Richard's ashes. We had chosen Shawford Down, a place Richard loved, and near where he was born. We prayed together, and then John left us to scatter the ashes under the trees.

The very next day was the Autistic Society picnic in the vicarage garden – another event I couldn't have got through without John.

A rash which Alec developed, and which all but stopped him doing his DIY, was declared to be 'general dermatitis of nervous origin'. I was so worried about him, but comforted that he kept coming to church and apparently turning to God for help. I prayed daily that he might be as aware as I was that 'underneath are the ever-lasting arms'. To protect him a little, we got a doctor's note to exempt him from jury service, for which he had just been summoned, and also postponed the hernia operation twice.

That summer I went very proudly to see Pips graduate from the Royal College of Music, and she came home with us for the holidays, having planned to go to teacher's training college the next year. I was so happy for her, and yet so desolate about Paul, who never mentioned Richard once.

I kept coming up against memories of Richard, such as his books which he kept in the wardrobe of the van. My knees buckled as I stood there, looking at them, and I sat down for a quiet cry. His reading had never improved much beyond the level of an eight-year-old, but it still gave him a lot of pleasure. Counting, on the other hand, never went beyond three. It didn't seem to matter all that much. One weekend I asked him what he had been doing at his unit.

'Putting candles in boxes,' he announced proudly.

'How many did you have to put in?' I was intrigued.

'Don't know,' he admitted with cheerful resignation.

'How did you know when to stop?'

'Box full!'

Silly Mummy. Now, at this memory, was it silly to cry? Was I crying because he was so retarded? No. For many years now, his limitations had just been part of his personality, and his episodes of violence like something imposed from outside. The Richard I knew was just so warm, loving and appreciative. I missed him terribly.

Eventually, Alec went in for his hernia operation. He wasn't too keen on hospitals, and obviously expected a gloomy time of it. This was proved quite wrong by one man who was the life and soul of the ward, and kept up a sense of fun all the time Alec was in. I was encouraged that he enjoyed this and wasn't irritated by it as he might have been. It seemed a sign that he was coming to terms with life again.

Also, to my great joy, he decided to take Communion while in hospital, and was so strengthened in his spirit by this, that he said he would take it at home when he got back. He gained his physical strength rapidly as well. Tears of bitter joy squeezed past my eyelids as we knelt at the altar rail together for practically the first time since our early days of marriage. Joy, because he was there. Bitter, because of what had brought him there.

# CHAPTER TWELVE

The habit of not questioning Alec about his faith was very difficult to shake off. After years of trying very hard not to push him, my reaction to this spiritual thaw was to be even more careful not to destroy a tentative beginning. It was not that he had ever doubted the existence of God as such, but religion had always been such a puzzle to him, and he felt that Christians got out of answering his questions by saying, 'God is a mystery.' This was such a frustration to him that he had given up asking the questions at all.

Certainly it was hard for him to square a God of love with what had been happening to his family through all these years. My own faith, which looked to God for support rather than blaming him, only served to irritate Alec. Occasionally he would become very anti-church, and although he tried not to take it out on me, his diary left no room for doubt. One week in particular he was obviously near bursting point.

*Sunday:* Una got up at 7 am – she gets fanatical on a Sunday.

*Wednesday:* Una dashed off to another of her church meetings.

*Friday:* Despite my not sanctioning her doing Sunday school duties (she has by all standards enough on her plate already) she's been intrigued into Friday night sessions – a very crafty move. These parsons have all kinds of guile at their finger tips.

What actually happened here was the beginning of the Anchor Club, which was a sort of Sunday school on Friday night, largely so that the choir boys should have some Christian teaching at their own level. You would think from the way Alec saw it that they moved it to Friday just to involve me. Needless to say I was one of many helpers, and it never seemed to occur to him that I could actually enjoy what I was doing.

Yet somehow, over the years, Alec had come to associate with the sufferings of Christ on the cross. The three-hour-long service which we always had in our church on Good Friday was something he seldom missed. A couple of years before, one of these services had obviously had a profound effect on him. Usually he would only go for one hour of the three, and in this case he went to the first hour at twelve o'clock, so I expected him back for dinner early. As the hours ticked by I went through the stage of telling myself not to worry, through the decision that I wouldn't let myself worry for another half hour, and at half past three was just beginning to get down to some serious worrying when he appeared.

He was still obviously very moved, having stayed the whole three hours. Clearly it had given him a lot to think about, and he admitted, 'I've never heard such preaching – I just could not leave.' The preacher was Alan Harrison, whom we had already come to love and respect, but Alec had of course not heard him preach before.

The only other time I had felt that God had really

penetrated the barriers Alec put up was quite unexpected. One Saturday when Alec was between jobs in his
DIY, and a chilly March wind thoughtfully gave way to
the warmest sunshine of the year, we decided to give ourselves a breather for a day. It seemed a long time since the
last holiday, and really we needed regular breaks to
forget the pressures of our situation.

First we went to a nature reserve on the marshes, and
Alec was very interested in all the various kinds of sea
birds, while I sat just soaking up the peace of the setting
– wind moving across the grasses, sunlight on water and
the unhurried haunting call of the birds. On days like
these I remembered so clearly the days of our early marriage, and sometimes it was as if all the hard times in
between hadn't happened. Watching him now talking to
the warden with his binoculars scanning the marshes, I
was just so grateful to see Alec relaxed and happy,
because I knew that without him carrying the emotional
and practical burden with me, I just could not have survived. He was a tall, wiry figure, his face was lined, and his
limp was still very much in evidence – but looking at him
I saw a man of immense strength.

After the marshes, we went to a Roman villa nearby.
Usually in places like this Alec would get around faster
than me, because I liked to look at the exhibits in detail.
To my surprise, I suddenly realised that Alec was some
way behind me, looking intently at a small glass cabinet I
had missed.

'Look,' he said, and then cleared a husky throat. 'Just
look at those nails.'

Inside the cabinet were a handful of Roman nails,
about five inches long, with square shafts. I must have
looked puzzled, because he added, 'About 40 AD, it says.'
Then, spelling it out because I was still struggling to catch
up with his train of thought, 'It was probably nails like
these that they used to crucify Christ.'

He stood there for several minutes more, almost as

though the nails had fixed him to the spot. I moved quietly, not wanting to disturb him, but as soon as he felt me move away, he followed me. I thanked God that he had somehow reached Alec that day, but I didn't want to intrude on this, and never felt I could bring up the subject of those nails again with Alec. That year Alec suggested that we should go to the three-hour Good Friday service together, and I just felt so blessed to be sitting beside Alec in church that I found it difficult to concentrate.

On Easter Sundays, however, I just had to recognise that there was no joy there for Alec. He simply couldn't make the connection. He sometimes understood that God was sharing our pain with us, but there seemed to be no victory either in the resurrection or in our problems. God might be love, but he had no power as far as Alec was concerned.

Christmas held even less meaning for him. It was just an immense waste of DIY time. He was at home, but wasn't allowed to get out the tools and make a mess because of people calling. Instead he had to sit around and talk, and his appetite for this was very small. By the end of the holiday I could feel him writhing with frustration, which found vent in the diary.

*Christmas Day:* Spent day avoiding treading on everybody, fetching coal, eating, washing up, wasting time. Two of Pips' friends came in the evening and we played silly games.

In fact, you would say that if Alec had any religion, it was his DIY. From the moment we moved into the rather delapidated house, it was an obsession. At first I shared it with him: this was to be our little nest, and there was so much to be done that neither of us could think of very much else. Because there was never a lot of money, we always had to do things ourselves, slowly and cheaply. But after the first few months, once I was basically comfortable, my attention wandered off to what I thought of as

106

life, like getting to know people and joining things.

For Alec, however, the next twenty years were one non-stop house improvement campaign. There wasn't a surface in the house that hadn't been treated, painted, shelved, wired or plastered, and sometimes all of those at various times. I knew that this was all for us, that he wanted us to have every convenience, and the house to be as modern and as beautiful as he could make it for us. Certainly he had some ingenious ideas, such as building a cupboard around the hot water pipes just deep enough to have a rail for drying tea-towels against the pipes. Yet the house was too small to have one room or another constantly full of tools and building materials, and he was a meticulous rather than speedy workman. It seemed so mean to complain about the mess, and to beg him to do more with us, but I often felt I could scream.

Apart from anything else, I knew that he was often struggling against pain and discomfort, and I wished he would tackle something less strenuous. Colds and stomach problems which would have sent others to bed with no sense of guilt were, for Alec, just a problem which you took to work with you until you dropped. In vain did I suggest that if he had a day off before it got too bad it would be over quicker. He hated going to a doctor, so many pains remained without explanation.

One November he decided to lay a concrete floor in the garage, which meant taking out many buckets of earth, loading them into the van and getting them down to the dump. It took several trips. Then he started on the concrete floor. It seemed to be going very slowly, and it was only from his diary I learned of the pain he was in.

*November 24th.* Persistent discomfort from stomach, has been three weeks now. Symptoms — soreness deep within my stomach to north-west of breast bone with sort of sympathetic tenderness below my swallowing mechanism and inclination continuously to swallow saliva.

In every way, Alec was a fighter. Life was hard, but it wasn't going to get him down without a struggle. Perhaps he had always felt that to surrender to God would have been to capitulate to weakness, and he would lose his driving force. Yet to me, God was my driving force, my source of strength, my only hope for the future.

Richard's death precipitated a change in Alec which seemed dramatic, but it was quite difficult to know what lay behind it. Just because he had learned to accept God's strength through the Communion didn't automatically mean that he was leaning on God all the time. There was talk of moving Alec's department of the factory to Winchester, and this worried him sick, as he felt he couldn't cope with driving backwards and forwards each day. I wanted to ask him to pray with me about it, but somehow I couldn't, and he struggled on fretting about a situation which never occurred.

As Alec and I adjusted to Richard's absence, and Alec recovered from the hernia operation, things began to look up. Reports from Paul were an increasing source of encouragement to us both. One charge nurse even reported his behaviour as 'very good indeed'. I hadn't heard such praise ever before from Oldthorpe, and praised God that the occupational therapy was having the effect I had hoped for. One day we were allowed to look round the unit and see a Mrs Hargreaves in charge, who said that Paul was 'no trouble at all', and showed us lots of things he had made. Then the day before Alec returned to work we brought Paul home, with help of course, and we made a victoria sandwich together. He took it back in triumph to his villa, where the staff were quite astounded that he was able to make a cake. Gleefully he cut and shared it out all round, trying to be fair, but with enough ability at quantity estimating to made sure his piece was certainly no smaller than anyone else's!

After Alec returned to work, life settled down again

into a routine of visits to Paul, autumn gardening for me, and DIY for Alec, but to my immense relief he did choose less strenuous jobs such as re-framing pictures. He even got someone to help him prune the fruit trees. As his confidence returned, however, he started painting the stairwell, and I despaired of ever making him recognise his limitations. His major worry was that Christmas was approaching, and he wasn't sure he could finish by then. This interruption seemed still to be the major significance of Christmas, and this puzzled me a lot. I had expected more understanding of what Christmas was about now that his faith had fallen back into place. Spiritual growth was apparently a very unpredictable phenomenon.

To his intense annoyance, just as it looked as though he could finish on time, Alec began to get a pain in his stomach. It seemed to me to be the result of the pressure he was putting upon himself. He came to church on Sunday morning, but was so concerned to get the sandpaper out the moment we returned that Pips and I decided we should bow to the inevitable and help him. At first he seemed reluctant to accept help, but with a sigh of relief we finished by tea time. Now we could look forward to a quiet evening.

'Do you mind if I leave the dishes to you two?' Alec asked as he left the table. 'I'd like to wash down the hall ceiling so it's ready for the lining paper.' Pips and I stared at him in amazement. But he did it, even though he was so exhausted when he finished that he went straight to bed.

The next day after work I insisted he went to the doctor, as the pain was increasing. His heartbeat was too fast, according to the doctor, but he thought the pain was due to having ricked himself while working. Alec, who knew it was nothing to do with the work, felt it was connected to the anxiety about possibly having to work in Winchester. In the days before Christmas the pain grew worse and worse. He could eat very little, and sleep was difficult too. I gave him Complan each night. When we went back to the doctor we got some medicine, but the pain was still increasing, so we went back again. This time the doctor began to suspect a stomach ulcer and changed the prescription.

So we came to Christmas, but it was a hard time for both of us. We missed Richard terribly, and Alec was fighting the pain bravely but didn't seem to be winning. By dint of resting all Christmas Eve, he managed to come to Midnight Communion with me, and for the first time felt the spiritual impact of what Christmas was all about. The festivities at home were still no more than a nuisance to him, and indeed no one really had their heart in it anyway. Alec could only eat a very light meal on Christmas Day, and spent part of the day in bed.

Although I had anticipated that the first Christmas without Richard would be hard, I had hoped that we could put it behind us and begin to look to a more hopeful future. Instead, I now had to face the fact that storm clouds were building up on the horizon.

'Hold me, Lord,' I prayed. 'I'm getting frightened again.'

# CHAPTER THIRTEEN

Paul couldn't come home for Christmas, but a church friend gave up the whole of Boxing Day so we could see him then. He was very good, and we went into a church to pray while we were on a walk, then took him back to his villa.

Over the next few days Alec got back to decorating the hall, getting up insulated wallpaper on the ceiling he had cleaned, but he wasn't really better, and had to keep stopping. He was able to eat so little, and his sleep was so disrupted, I wasn't at all surprised. For another couple of weeks I prayed for him to get better, and when he was referred to a specialist I began to hope that they would find a real reason for the pain so they could do something. Meanwhile another medicine had been prescribed, and this seemed to help.

For the first time, it looked as though Paul was going to miss the annual Autistic Society party because Alec just could not manage the drive. Then someone in church realised that this was likely to happen and arranged for two people to help, one driver and one back-up, so that Paul could come. He had such a lovely time that I really didn't know how to thank my friends. For that day at least I could forget for a while my worries about Alec.

The following Sunday he couldn't face church, and was so touched by the messages I brought back with me, as well as by the number of people who said they were glad to see him back when he managed to go the next week. He was now established as a member of the congregation in his own right, which was lovely for him.

The specialist moved into top gear when Alec saw him, and ordered X-rays and a barium meal for a few days' time. While we waited for the results, the pain really wasn't too bad, and Alec was managing at work very well. Then he undertook moving more rubble in the back garden, which set him back a lot. For some time now he had been eating no more than a little porridge at breakfast, soup at mid-day and bread and milk before bed. He began to look so thin and gaunt, and I felt as though I woke up praying for him and just prayed all day until I fell asleep. A wonderful reassurance came from this, that God loved us both, had brought us this far, and would look after the future. It was surprisingly easy to trust a God who was so real to me. I kept looking for hopeful signs, and seeing them.

But there were also terrible moments when I saw that, overall, Alec was going downhill. One Sunday he spent a lot of time in bed, then got up to watch a television programme he liked, and had to give up half way through as he felt too ill. I helped him back into bed and he just flopped down in relief, too weak even to brush away the tear which slipped down his cheek. Sometimes I thought I would give anything just to be able to cry, but I knew this wouldn't help him, and I really wanted to be strong for him.

Finally, the X-ray results came through and it seemed that there was nothing wrong with the digestive system, so they were now going to investigate the gall bladder. Alec insisted on going to work through all this, and still gave priority to taking Paul out and getting to church. One Saturday, I persuaded him that we needed a trip out just for the two of us. In fact, I simply wanted to be in the countryside. We didn't drive far, and I just felt the peace reaching through to me as we lay on the grass listening to the birds. I could hear my heart beat, and when the sun came out, it was like feeling a touch from God even though my eyes were closed. I sat up and looked around me at the wonderful blue of the sky and fresh greens of spring. Then I looked down at Alec, asleep for a moment, but with the lines of pain still etched on a face which had become so thin. The sunlight made the shadows of the lines all the stronger, and as I looked at him, fear stabbed into me.

'Oh God,' I prayed desperately, 'don't let him go on suffering like this. Help the doctors to find out quickly what is wrong.' Yet now I realised I was not only longing to know, but afraid to know as well.

The next day he managed to go to church again, saying that he really missed worship if he didn't go. We also took Paul out, and since the vicar was with us, had a little service of anointing for healing for Paul, which I found very moving.

During the next week Alec was told his gall bladder would have to be operated on in three or four weeks. He felt such hope at this, thinking that after the operation he would be fine again, and I supported him because he needed the hope so much. Over the next week the pain became steadily worse, and then he became jaundiced. Eventually the surgery became a matter of urgency, and he was rushed into hospital. I sat with him in the ambulance, as we told each other the sooner it was over the better.

Indeed, immediately after the operation I could see that the jaundice was gone, but he was in a lot of pain still, so I left him to sleep. Called into the Sister's office, I was surprised to see the surgeon and the house doctor.

'Do have a seat, Mrs Menniss,' someone suggested, and I sat down, looking up at the people for whom there weren't enough seats. Suddenly I felt very small and vulnerable, and afraid of what they were going to say. I had been told bad news so many times in my life I knew the signs.

'Please just tell me,' I said, as calmly as I could. The surgeon sat down and looked into my eyes.

'We were able to remove a block from your husband's gall bladder, which sorted out the jaundice,' he began, 'but the blockage turned out to be a growth on the pancreas which was also affecting the liver. All the signs are that it is cancerous. There is no more we can do for him. I'm very sorry.'

'How long...?' I couldn't finish.

'If he makes a good recovery from the operation, perhaps six to twelve months. Or he may just go downhill from here and only live another few weeks.'

This was it, then. I steeled myself against emotion. I only needed to know one more thing.

'Does he know?'

'No. He just knows we have by-passed a blockage.' I paused, arrowed a prayer for wisdom, and decided.

'Please don't tell him anything more. I'll come back tomorrow.'

Somehow I walked to the bus stop, and was relieved that a bus came very quickly. I held my panic and pain at arm's length until I was walking past the vicarage, when I suddenly knew that the sympathy I would find there was just what I needed. John and Joy were so gentle with me, prayed with me, and insisted that I stay the night. I didn't sleep very much, but it was immeasurably better than it would have been at home, alone. In the morning they helped me to pray and compose myself to visit Alec.

'You must come in on your way home each night,' said

114

Joy. I protested, but soon felt that these visits were the only thing that kept me from complete breakdown. I felt enveloped in their love.

After ten days, Alec was returned home. He was able to come downstairs on crutches for part of each day, and I spent every possible moment with him. We watched a little television, and listened to music, and I read to him quite a bit. A book about the countryside in Britain gave such lovely descriptions that we felt we were there looking at it ourselves. We also prayed, increasingly as time went by. Alec was fascinated by the story of the early church as told in Acts, and I read a few verses every day. On Sundays either John, the vicar, or his curate, brought us Communion immediately after the service, which gave us a real sense of belonging to the parish family. Always they would read a gospel passage to us, and one day John read Jesus' words, 'I am the bread of life.' Then as Alec received the sacrament a look of wonder lit up his face and he said, 'I have received the bread of life!' But the contrast between his spiritual and physical condition was becoming daily greater.

Alec had painkillers every four hours, but often needed them before the next dose was due, enduring an hour of increasing pain before he could take any more. At night I slept on a camp bed in his room so I could give him his tablet at ten and then set the alarm for two o'clock. He was often in great pain before I could give him another tablet, but tried not to wake me before the alarm. At two, I would give him the tablet with a warm drink, and I would pray and sing for him while he waited for the tablet to take effect. Often I sang the 'Te Deum' – 'We praise thee, O God' – and he would fall asleep as the pain receded. By six o'clock he was in pain again, and I would make a cup of tea for his next tablet. He had no interest in food, and a few spoonfuls was all he ever managed in one day.

Pips came home from college during April, and I could

see that she knew the situation was quite bad. I just had to tell her that her dad might never get better.

'Oh,' she paused, reeling from the reality of the news. 'Poor Mum.'

I often asked God whether it would be right to mention the word 'cancer' to Alec, but I was quite sure I shouldn't. I also felt it was right to go on praying that a miracle would save him.

At the beginning of May Alec asked that there should be a healing service held for him. A group of our closest Christian friends gathered around Alec in our dining room, with our vicar, John Hobbs and Chris Atkins, brother of the previous curate, who had taken his place. We joined hands in a circle, and Chris laid hands on Alec, praying for his healing. Then John anointed him with oil, and gave a blessing. We all sat in silence for a while, then each of our friends in turn kissed Alec and silently went out.

The sense of the presence of Christ was so powerful that neither Alec nor I could speak for over an hour. Then the doorbell rang, and it was one of the sisters from the convent who came to tell us that while we were having our little service, the sisters had been praying in their chapel. We felt that the silence could not have been broken in a better way.

Alec startled me the next day by putting on his artificial leg. He seemed to have gained strength, and I dared to believe he would be healed. In the afternoon, he asked Pips to start the engine of the Dormobile for a little while so that it didn't seize up. She went out to try, but came back looking quite upset, and said, 'It won't start for me, only for Dad.'

Astonished, I watched Alec walk out to the garage, get into the driver's seat and start the engine. He told Pips to get in beside him, then backed out of the garage and drove round the local streets for a few minutes. Pips wasn't sure about disturbing his grim look of concentration, but as soon as he put on the handbrake again, she couldn't help exclaiming, 'Good God!'

'You are absolutely right,' Alec grinned at her. 'It is good God!'

We thanked God together for this new strength, and prayed hourly for his healing. Our hopes were short-lived, as he began to deteriorate fast. Yet the miracle I asked for was granted in the completeness of Alec's spiritual healing. The last vestiges of doubt he had over the years were gone, and God was so real to him that I felt he was way above me spiritually. Although I continued to pray for a miracle of physical healing, I had a sense that he was already half-way to heaven.

One day, Alec asked me to read the wedding service aloud to him. How I got through the passage 'till death us do part' I don't know. Within a week he needed to be back in hospital, and I resumed my daily visits to him there. Pips came down the next day, and Alec rallied for her, assuring her that she should concentrate on her exams and not try to come home again until they were over.

In hospital, the chaplain brought us both Communion. Afterwards, we sat there holding hands.

'Well, Una, do you think I can still get better?'

'Of course you can,' I said steadily.

'You never give up, do you?' Alec replied with a smile.

Once again, my visits to the vicarage held me together on my trips back to the empty house. John and Joy prayed with me, and without them I couldn't have kept going. Alec's concentration was now very slight, but we still read Acts together. After a week, Sister told me there was nothing more they could do.

'I understand,' I replied. 'I will just go on praying.'

'Yes, do,' she replied. 'We have seen miracles happen in this very hospital.'

Yet within two days Alec was looking so bad, and was in such pain, that I went to the chapel and prayed, 'O God, if there is not to be a notable miracle, please take Alec to yourself soon.'

Next day he was visibly worse, and I wasn't surprised the next morning when Sister phoned to say I should come as soon as I could. I was supposed to be waiting for my brother to collect me, but he was coming from some way away, so I set off for the hospital by myself. I was met by the chaplain, and knew that Alec was gone.

There was a service of Communion starting immediately, and I just knew I had to go. To be given this means of strength at just that point was a wonderful provision of God for me.

Afterwards I was taken to his stepmother, who was waiting for me, and we went together to the mortuary. I was full of fear, and didn't want to go. But as soon as I saw his face, so utterly at peace, I was able to release him.

I knew he was with his Lord, and free from all suffering at last.

# CHAPTER FOURTEEN

Unable to cope with the fact of Alec's death, my mind closed in upon itself. I was numb, and there was so much to do. Alec's stepmother was staying with me, cooking meals and making sure I ate them, while my brother Denis helped with business matters, but there were some agonising decisions that I had to face alone.

Pips was still taking her final exams, and would not finish for another few days. Should she be told that her father had died? I knew as I made this decision that whatever I did, I would probably wish later that I had done the opposite. On balance, I decided that to fail her exams would cause such enormous long-term practical problems, that she had better not know yet. I had to risk her feeling betrayed.

A close friend offered to go up to London and break the news to her on the evening after the last exam. Poor Pips opened the door, saw who it was, and crumpled.

'Dad's dead, isn't he?'

The college allowed her to come home for three

weeks, and at last we could grieve openly together. There were no more secrets. All sense of meaning seemed to have drained out of my life, but Pips was there, and a great comfort to me.

And, as always, the phrases from the Bible, which had helped me through so many a crisis, strengthened me again now. I knew that the 'everlasting arms of God' were supporting me, saving me from a headlong plunge into the pit of depression which seemed so close. Again and again the joy Alec had come to know came vividly into my mind, even while I was thinking of the pain he went through. If Alec had been physically healed by my prayers and had still not found God, that would have been harder to accept in some ways than his death. And who is to say which is the greater miracle? No, even in my grief I could praise God for the spiritual healing which had come to Alec, and for the certainty I had that he was now with Jesus, as he had so longed to be at the end.

Since Communion had become so precious to Alec, it was agreed that we should not just organise the usual burial service, but make it a Communion of Thanksgiving for Alec's life and for God's revelation of himself to Alec. Many relations and friends came, including some from Alec's factory. Chris gave an address, telling of Alec's pilgrimage in search of Christ, which was rewarded in the last weeks of his life, culminating in the ultimate revelation when Christ welcomed him face to face. It was an uplifting moment in a sea of turmoil and sobbing.

When Pip returned to college for the last week of term, I went to stay with Roger and Diana Atkins, the former curate who had now returned from Australia. It was so good to be in a Christian home, and I began to learn a very important lesson about suffering. Roger found a widow crying in his church one morning, and I was able to help so much just by crying with her. Perhaps even my pain could be offered to God and be used by him.

This was the first of several breaks which helped me to

adjust to being alone and still able to enjoy something. It was quite a painful process, like learning to walk again on a shattered knee-joint, and my first steps were very tentative. It didn't seem to be getting any easier, but I was spending a week on the Suffolk coast in a caravan with Denis and Phyllis when a silly competition suddenly became fun, and I realised that, until now, I had forgotten how to laugh.

Pip and a friend took me camping in Wales, and I found the emptiness and pain receding as I looked at the majestic strength of the mountains and the timeless sea stretching beyond my sight. God's thoughts were so much bigger than mine, and his purposes so loving. Through the many years when Alec had rebuffed any attempt I made to share my faith with him, God had given me peace so that I should not fret about it, and faith to believe that the situation would change. If I had given up on Alec, or made him feel he was falling short, he could never have gone on supporting me through the apparently unending struggle which drained us so. His love, although sometimes expressed in ways I didn't altogether appreciate – such as the non-stop house-improvement scheme – was strong, practical and constant. And at the end, had God not been vindicated? So I could trust now, despite the confusion of my emotions and the sense of being abandoned, that God had more plans for my good in the future.

Pips returned home to live, having been offered a job teaching the trumpet in a few surrounding schools. For both of us, this stability was good. I would have found it hard to live alone. Now we could begin to build a new normality together.

Of course, with Alec I had also lost the necessary transport to visit Paul. Many men in the church offered to take me over every other week. Sometimes he even came home. For many, this sacrifice of hours at the weekend was no easy task, but I tried to show them just how much

I appreciated it, and trust that God blessed them for their concern for myself and Paul. They could not have been blamed for feeling they were witnessing a desolate and hopeless situation. It often felt like that to me. Paul never missed 'Daddy', never spoke of him. I was glad he was spared the sadness of death, but oh, how it hurt!

Early in September Roger's brother Chris, who had given Alec's funeral address, asked me to stay for a week-end with himself and Angela. While I was there, they asked me to go with them to a Christian meeting at a place called Post Green.

'It might be rather different from what you have come across before,' explained Chris. 'Have you heard anything about "the baptism in the Spirit"?'

'The words sound as though I ought to,' I puzzled. 'It sounds sort of old and new at the same time. I give up. You'd better tell me.'

Chris laughed. 'You've just about summed it up, in some ways. I don't need to tell you, Una, of all people, that you have God's Spirit in you. You have been guided and strengthened by him for many years. That's the old bit.

'The new bit, which is what these people at Post Green have discovered, along with many others, is that you can ask God to fill you totally with his Spirit, to empower you in a new way. Sometimes the experience is overwhelming, and sometimes just a quiet confirmation of the joy and faith you already have. Either way, it adds up to a changed life, because Jesus seems so much nearer. To me, it felt as though my Christian life was given a whole new dimension, and it is certainly revolutionising my parish as people open up to God in this way. At Post Green is a whole community of people who have come together to explore God's love for them in the light of this experience. Would you like to go and see for yourself?'

I was intrigued. If God had anything good to give, I knew I couldn't refuse.

The meeting was crowded, and the people very loving, but oh so noisy! They lifted their arms as they sang choruses I didn't know, and everything felt so strange. Then Jean Darnall spoke, and I suddenly understood what they were so excited about. I had never expressed my love for God so exuberantly, but theirs was the same wonderful God as mine. By the end of the meeting I was at least on the same wavelength. Over coffee afterwards, a young woman spoke to me again about the baptism in the Spirit, and I tried to explain what I felt, which was difficult because I hardly knew myself. Then Chris came over, and they prayed together that I would be filled with the Spirit. Something in me longed to know God in this way, but I was terrified that I might start praying and worshipping in a strange language. I had heard this in the meeting, and it seemed so alien. To my relief, nothing dramatic happened.

During the weeks that followed, Chris remained a great support. I saw through him how the whole congregation in his parish was empowered and renewed by this release of the Spirit in their lives, and increasingly, I felt God was calling me to accept the gifts he was holding out to me.

As the year moved on, I had increasing peace about Alec and the spiritual healing he had known. I read that Jesus said, 'Father, I want them with me – those you've given me – so that they can see my glory,' and I knew without doubt that Alec was with Jesus, seeing his glory.

Christmas, however, was very difficult. It was only last year that Alec had begun to appreciate the spiritual meaning of it all, and made the great effort in his weakness to come to the Midnight Communion with me. This year it was I who found it so difficult to go. We did all the right things: decorations, festive food, all the trimmings. Paul came home with two Mauritian nurses from his villa. He seemed happy, and I was reassured. I managed to look merry, I think, but the very effort of pretending made me realise the emptiness I was hiding.

The next six months, as the numbness lifted, seemed to be a series of ups and downs. I had some lovely breaks with friends, a trip to Paris, visits from people I loved, and I began to find new roles to fill my time. I gave several talks for the Autistic Society, and joined the committee of the Eastleigh Society for the Mentally Handicapped.

On the negative side, I was oppressed by Paul's situation. I constantly needed help to visit him, I had to be very cautious about being left alone with him because his behaviour was so unpredictable, and I was increasingly worried by the lack of occupation he was getting. In May I heard that his villa was in isolation due to some infection, and that none of the men had been able to go to the Special Training Unit. I was afraid that the frustration of being confined to the villa might have set off some of the 'difficult' behaviour which had been increasing recently. A sense of frustration burnt in me: was there no purpose to his life at all? It was a struggle to believe God was in control, but somehow I held on.

Then, in the middle of May, this belief was rocked to its foundations.

David Moore, the social worker at Oldthorpe, came to see me. I knew from his eyes that it was bad news, and I made him a cup of tea to delay the moment of knowing.

'I'm afraid there's been trouble with Paul, Mrs Menniss. There was some delay yesterday morning in letting Paul out of his room to get dressed. He must have felt he was being left there.' He sighed, not knowing how to go on. My heart groaned in pain at the picture I could paint around the simplicity of his words. Paul, my Paul, standing at the door of his cell, peering in desperation through the toughened glass peep-hole, his understanding clouded and his emotions in turmoil. Trapped, alone, abandoned.

'He just bashed his face against the glass in the door until he broke it, and his nose. I'm afraid he's in a bad way.'

The social worker had been looking down at his hands as he spoke. Now when I apparently didn't react, he glanced up at me swiftly. I sat shock-still, drained of colour. He went on, nervously now, and watching me.

'Of course, we've taken him to hospital for treatment. He's back now with some pain killers and extra sedation, just in case. We've kept him in the same room, but of course we've had to board up the window. He doesn't seem to mind.' Every word he spoke was like the blow of a hammer, but still I sat with a slack jaw, unable to give expression to the screams and sobs within. Reassured by my silence, he tackled the next difficult issue.

'You'll understand, of course, that we can't just carry on as if this never happened. The nursing staff are demanding that he be sent to Rampton, and I really think this would be best for everybody. I've brought a form for you to sign giving permission for the transfer.'

Rampton! All I knew about Rampton was that I wouldn't be able to visit.

'What if I refuse?' My voice was toneless.

David cleared his throat. 'I don't think that would be a good idea, Mrs Menniss. The hospital will simply take you to court to get an order overruling your refusal. I'm sorry.'

I was as trapped as Paul. There was nowhere to turn. I knew, with an agonising certainty, that I must not sign that form. It meant betrayal, agony for me, and how much worse for Paul. Yet I apparently had no choice. Also I wanted to get this man, who I knew meant me no harm, out of my house. I signed the form, and he disappeared, probably as grateful to go as I was to shut the door behind him. Then the horror swept over me, like physical pain, and my knees buckled. I sobbed and sobbed. It was as if a third member of my family had died. If I couldn't see Paul, he might as well be dead.

# CHAPTER FIFTEEN

For a long while my mind, thrashing around in pain, could not focus on any one thought, but eventually I cried myself out. As my sobs subsided, the thing uppermost in my mind was that I had done wrong in signing that transfer form, and that I should find some way to overrule the official procedures. Pain and anger had blocked God from my mind, but now I asked him for peace and guidance, and as I did this, my frustration turned to determination. I remembered the doctor who had helped to get occupational therapy for Paul five years ago, and spent some time tracking him down. His horror at my situation, and his sympathy, were consoling, but I knew I had done the right thing two days later when he phoned back.

'I've spoken to a solicitor friend of mine, who says you must have legal help. He is happy to do this for you free of charge.' Not only did I know a loving God, who gave me strength and peace, but a mighty God who could work through people I didn't know. Not that I saw the results yet.

Day after day Paul was locked in his room. When someone took me to visit him I was locked in with him. I always took games to play, and some books to look at, and he was pleased to see me. Yet even after I got used to the bruising on his face, I was horrified by his appearance. Heavily drugged, and with nothing to do all day, he looked as though his spirit had been crushed. The hospital administration called it 'treatment by seclusion'.

A few days later my brother visited me, and he and Phyllis came over with me to see Paul. This time the nurse opened his door and put a table across the doorway so we could sit around that and talk to him from the other side. As long as the villa staff received orders that he was to be locked in, they were powerless to do anything else. He seemed quite calm, but looked terrible. Denis and Phyllis took me home, but wouldn't stay for a cup of tea. Denis told me later that they drove round the corner, then pulled up out of my sight and both cried and cried.

Paul had now become the focus of a union issue among the nurses, and those belonging to one union wouldn't work with him, demanding that he be sent to Rampton. I had explained the situation to my newly-acquired solicitor, and he had written to the hospital saying that I had signed the consent form in a state of shock and distress, and now withdrew my consent. He also asked them for details of how Paul's time was occupied. I had written on this subject before, and had a very evasive reply to the effect that they did what they could for him. Their answer to the solicitor was more detailed, and confirmed my fears. Paul was allowed to 'relax' or 'watch television' for six hours every day and all weekend. I knew he didn't show much interest in television and I read 'relax' as 'vegetate'. Still, the support of the solicitor meant I was now dealing with hard facts, and I felt I could face any possibility of legal action with him beside me.

To my surprise, the administration at Rampton helped my cause by refusing to have Paul, as did three other hospitals in the area. As far as they were concerned, there was no particular reason for moving him, so the staff where he was had to accept the situation. Actually, Paul became more settled, and the union nurses backed down to the extent of dealing with him. Even better, Paul was given permission to resume his sessions at the training unit, and after initial resistance from him, was soon happily occupied there.

This state of affairs was now bearable, but only just, and in July I had an interview with a Senior Nursing Officer, pleading for longer hours of occupation for Paul, particularly that he should be given exercise to use up his energy. I said I was convinced that at least some of his difficult behaviour was due to the frustration of being idle so much of the time. He was silent as I came out with my much-rehearsed request, but I couldn't make his eyes meet mine. Then when I petered into silence, he gave me a long, hard look, and delivered what I saw as the 'official line'.

'I do appreciate your concern, Mrs Menniss, but you must realise that we have a great deal of experience in these matters, and I cannot agree with you. A patient like Paul will always be prone to violent episodes, with patches of good behaviour in between. Whether he is occupied or not has no bearing on the matter.'

'But several of the nurses have said that Paul has loads of intelligence if only it could be harnessed, and anyone can see that he is younger and stronger than the other patients in the villa. His needs are quite different, surely.'

'We do what we can to take this sort of thing into account, of course, but this must be secondary. While Paul's behaviour is so unpredictable we simply must be sure that he is in a protected environment at all times. I don't have to spell out to you that he is capable at a moment's notice of physically harming either the staff or himself. I assure you that his seclusion is for his own good.'

I was silent, having no more ammunition, yet knowing in my heart that he was wrong. If they would only trust him more. If they would just give him the dignity of a human being I was sure that Paul would live up to it. Every day I prayed for improvement in his situation, and was increasingly sure that God was going to work. For the next three months I prayed on.

Although I had discovered new depths in my prayer life since praying for the baptism in the Spirit, I found myself wanting something more. Half of me now felt that I needed the gift of tongues to pray effectively in this 'hopeless' situation, but I was still afraid.

I spent a fortnight in September visiting various friends in the Midlands. One couple took me to a Christian musical celebration called 'Come Together', and I was very moved by the large choir, even though I didn't know the songs they were singing. When the evangelist leading the evening announced a time of intercession, with an opportunity for special prayer requests to be made known to him, I knew this was for me. I explained Paul's complex story and my anxieties about him as simply as I could. With everyone in the church holding hands, the evangelist prayed that God would intervene in Paul's life to bring about healing and richness of life. I was overwhelmed and in tears. Six hundred Christians united in prayer for my Paul! God's love was very real.

The last six days of my holiday were spent with Roger and Diana Atkins. I talked to them about my desire to know more of God's Spirit, but said that my fear of 'tongues' was keeping me from actually asking for it. The morning I was to leave, I came down to find a book by my breakfast plate.

'What's this?' I called out to Diana in the kitchen. She came in and put the marmalade on the table.

'We thought it might help with some of your questions, and sort out those fears you were talking about,' she said in a reassuringly straightforward manner. I picked it up.

'The Holy Spirit and You' I read aloud. 'Well, you can't get more direct than that. Who are Dennis and Rita Bennett?'

'Why don't you read it on the train?' smiled Diana.

I did just that and was immediately absorbed. As I finished it that night at home, I knelt by my bed and asked God to fill me with his Spirit and give me all that he had prepared for me. Immediately I found myself speaking a few words in a language I did not know, and in a few days this language became fluent. I was full of joy, all doubts dissolved. I knew that I was to use this gift to pray for Paul every day, and many times a day I would repeat quietly, 'I send forth, in the name of Christ, healing for Paul and guidance for all those who care for him.' Then I would add a prayer in the new language God had given me. I know now that this new power in my prayers marked the turning point for Paul. At the time, nothing gave any sign that this was the case.

Two weeks later, I heard that Paul had hit one of the nurses who belonged to the union which had objected to his continued presence in the past. They had withdrawn their labour from the villa, and were again demanding that Paul be sent to Rampton. From the way God had been leading me to pray I felt that this could not be his will, so my only reaction was to redouble my praying.

Then David Moore, who had first visited me with the request for the transfer, but who had been impressed with Paul's behaviour when occupied, let me know that a psychiatrist was to come from Rampton to consider Paul's case. I was able to discover the name and address of this woman, and there was just time for me to send her a history of Paul from my point of view, and to ask that I might see her on the day the future of my son was to be decided.

My previous experiences had led me to feel quite defensive about such people, but this psychiatrist put me at my ease immediately.

'I do hope you haven't had to wait very long, Mrs

Menniss. I'm sorry that I couldn't be more precise about the time I could see you, but I wanted to see everybody involved with Paul's case first, since I knew your feelings on the matter. You should understand that I don't make decisions, only recommendations. Having said that, you will be pleased to hear that Paul is not the kind of patient we have at Rampton.' How I praised and thanked God!

The battle was far from over, however. There was still a strong lobby to have Paul transferred to somewhere else, although one of the charge nurses said he found Paul's behaviour consistently steady, and that all the complaints came from the other shift. It was quite true that it was the other charge nurse who always greeted me with the story of some misdeed of Paul's. I had my suspicions about all this, but there was nothing I could do except pray as the administrative battle raged on. Certainly, Paul seemed to be steady and fairly happy, given his circumstances.

Early in December I received an invitation to a nativity play which was being performed by the trainees at Paul's Special Training Unit. I found it difficult to believe that Paul would be in this, and I phoned David Moore, who promised to find out. His letter in reply was a great cause for rejoicing:

'Since you telephoned I have been over to the Special Training Unit. The staff there were quite surprised when I asked about Paul's behaviour, as they have always found him to be co-operative and manageable. With regard to the nativity play, I understand that Paul is in fact playing an important role.'

Consequently I arrived for the play with high hopes, and was not disappointed. One of the staff read the story, and the trainees acted out the parts. I found it starkly beautiful and moving. Paul had given me few opportunities to feel proud of him in public. Now this made up for what I had not had in the past, and I was as thrilled as any play-school mum by the sight of Paul as an angel in a

132

long white robe with wings and a halo. He played his part perfectly.

Two days later there was a Christmas party in the villa to which families were invited. Pips and I went along, and were very impressed by the Christmassy atmosphere the staff had managed to create with a few decorations and party fare. After tea, percussion instruments were handed out, recorded music was switched on, and the patients played their various instruments with gusto. Paul played a drum, and was obviously delighted.

As I looked round, I couldn't help thinking that all the patients were more alert since they had started to visit the Special Training Unit each day. I thanked God that he had guided me to push for such facilities for Paul five years previously, because it had increased the richness of so many lives.

Christmas was very quiet: Paul came home on Boxing Day.

At 7.40 on January 1st I was woken by the phone. Rushing downstairs, I was into an unbelievable conversation before I had worked out what day it was.

'Mrs Menniss? You don't know me, but I'm the Divisional Nursing Officer at Oldthorpe. There is to be a meeting of all those concerned with Paul's welfare this morning. It has been proposed that he should have a proper programme of rehabilitation, with full occupation and more exercise, and that he should go home at weekends. Would you be prepared to have him home?'

'I ... I don't know,' I stammered. 'That is, of course I will.... It's just that I've never thought it would be possible to have him overnight now that my husband isn't here. I don't know what to say....'

Yet as I spoke, I saw this development as the answer to my prayers, and God seemed to be saying, 'I am sending him home, and I will be with you.' Even so, I couldn't imagine coping every weekend.

'I wonder if we could try every other weekend?' I

suggested. 'Just for a trial period?'

'I think that's a splendid idea, Mrs Menniss. I'll put that forward at the meeting, and of course we'll be sending you full details of the decisions taken. Thank you so much. Good-bye.'

Slowly, as I made my way towards the kettle, the implications of this conversation dawned on me. Until very recently, some of the nursing staff were maintaining that Paul was too unpredictable and violent to be handled by male nurses, and now they were sending him home to a middle-aged widow by herself! This could have made me very frightened. Yet I had firmly maintained that with exercise and activity, Paul's behaviour was stable. Now I was being made to demonstrate my trust in him.

Even more important, I was placing my trust in God. He had promised me that I would see his glory in Paul. Did I believe that the prayers of the six hundred people together had finally released God's power to action? Yes, I did. Had I not always known that my submission to the outpouring of God's Spirit in me had brought new power to my prayers?

And what of the prayer which had become as natural as breathing? 'I send forth, in the name of Christ, healing for Paul and guidance for all those who care for him.' Did I believe that God had been working on all those who dealt with Paul? What greater proof could I want than that telephone call? God had completely changed and enlightened their minds.

And if my prayers for the staff had been effective, must I not also believe that Paul himself was being healed? As surely as I prayed, he was being soothed out of his frustrations, his mind cleared to accept training, his heart softened with a new hope.

How my heart sang! Never had a year begun in such a blaze of glory!

# CHAPTER SIXTEEN

The doorbell rang, and I jumped, even though I had been waiting for it for the past hour. Paul had come. Was I ready? The house and the food had been organised for some time, but my mind was still twitching between joyful expectation, panic and prayer. With a deep breath and a strong sense of beginning a new era in my life, I opened the door.

There stood a friendly, thick-set ambulance man, for whom this was just the first job that Saturday morning.

'Mrs Menniss? We've got a very excited lad out here for you.' As he spoke, his mate opened the back door and Paul, not bothering with the steps, leapt out into the road and stood there, beaming. He was home.

'Paul!' He ran towards me and we met half-way down the path, where I gave him a big hug and a kiss, partly to hide the tears which I only just blinked back. He was a good head taller than I, and I had to look up at him as I chattered my way back into the house, my arm in his, revelling in his smile. At the door I turned to see the driver climbing back into the ambulance.

'Thank you so much!' I called out.

'Not at all, lady. You two just have a good time now. If there's any problems, phone the hospital. We'll be back tomorrow at five.' He slammed the door and they were off.

Somehow, his words seemed to emphasise that I was on my own. On my own? Never. I drew Paul into the kitchen and we sat down, holding hands across the formica table.

'Paul, I'm so happy. Shall we thank Jesus that you're home and ask him to help us have a good weekend?' Paul smiled and bowed his head. So began the first weekend, steeped in prayer for Paul, and started by prayer with Paul.

Everything had been planned with the smoothness of a military operation. First, coffee at home so he could get his bearings. He was no conversationalist, but he listened happily to what I was saying, and seemed to be fairly at peace with himself.

Then football on the vicarage lawn, to work out some of his energy. Watching him running, I could see how stiff he still was from the years of inactivity, and his shoulders were bowed from hours of sitting hunched up in a chair, rocking, rocking, rocking the weeks away. Through those years when I wasn't allowed to do very much about his situation, I had to swallow my indignation, but now that I was in the driving seat, the visible reminder of those years fired up my determination that from now on, his life would be better.

Home again, to find Pips and her new fiancé Graham busy in the kitchen. Graham came out to meet us in the hall.

'Hello Paul, old man. How are you? Dinner in ten minutes, OK? Why don't you go and wash your hands?' Graham hadn't known the family long, but was already at home with Paul. He asked questions which included him but didn't need any answers, and found just the right note of cheerful simplicity. As Paul headed for the stairs, Graham gave me an understanding smile.

'He's looking good, Una, and so are you. Is everything all right?' The concern in his dark eyes was very real, and yet he was so calm. What a rock, I found myself thinking. I'm glad he and Pips have decided to marry.

Pips blew in from the scullery balancing a salad bowl, a fistful of knives and forks, and four glasses.

'I've put tomatoes in, I hope that's all right, and does Paul like beetroot? I can't remember.' She unloaded onto the table. 'Hello, Mum.'

'Hello, Pips.' What a support they both were in their different ways. Above all, they were there.

Over dinner I found Paul rather jittery, with the tense excitement which I knew could easily turn sour, so he listened to a cassette of classical music on his bed for a while, and then fell asleep. I sat beside him, praying in tongues, and felt reassured. This weekend was God's doing. He wouldn't let me down.

Paul awoke completely calm and we went out for a long walk. The next day was to be my birthday, so we had a pre-birthday tea which Pips prepared. A few friends came round and played games, with which Paul joined in very happily. Although things were going so well, Graham offered to sleep in the house in case of trouble in the night. I was so grateful to him for the added sense of security, and we all slept well.

I was determined that from the first visit home Paul would join in worship in church if at all possible, so the next morning we went to Parish Communion. So many people there had been praying for Paul that he was greeted like a hero over coffee. Many knew him from helping with outings in the past. Since he was obviously coping with it all, I left him surrounded and found myself next to Joy Wood, a friend who was also watching him from a distance.

'What a special blessing it is to see Paul,' she

commented as she sipped her coffee.

'Thank you,' I smiled back. 'I hope his fidgeting and rocking didn't distract you too much. You were behind us, weren't you?'

'I was so moved to see him at the altar rail for a blessing that I nearly forgot to take Communion,' she grinned. 'No, Una, he was wonderfully good. I wouldn't have missed him being here for the world.'

'Just look at him beaming at everybody. Who would think he spent all his childhood so locked up in his own mind that he wouldn't have noticed anyone else?'

Joy nodded. 'Of course, I didn't know him then, but I can still see a big change. Well done, Una, you're winning.'

'Not me,' I reminded her. 'All of us, by our prayers.'

I was still marvelling after Paul had been collected by a nurse from the villa and gone off quite happily. Paul had been home to stay for the first time in fifteen years. It felt like God's birthday present to me, and the best I had ever been given.

That deep sense of gratitude stayed with me as the fortnightly visits began to fall into a pattern. The second visit home was just as successful and included the Autistic Society's party, where all was well. Every visit seemed to bring a new sense of accomplishment, not just that we had survived, but that some definite progress had been made. Mothers of 'normal' children don't realise how much they are taking for granted, and how much joy can be extracted from watching your son happily playing board games with others, even though the games are simplified and your son is twenty-eight years old.

It was almost as though Paul needed to remind me during the third visit just what a miracle I was seeing, by showing me a flash of the behaviour patterns of the past. On a walk he suddenly pinched my arm and gave a slight kick to my leg. Fear prickled up my back. There was no one around. I decided to say nothing and carry on walking, praying in tongues for all I was worth. Paul came along behind, and I didn't speak to him again until we reached a low wall from where we could look at the river. Then I took out the flask of tea and packet of biscuits – what we called a 'pretend picnic' – and from that moment all seemed to be calm again.

Some features of the weekend became regular spots, such as football on the vicarage lawn. It was so good of John Hobbs to let us come there, as the big stretch of grass surrounded by trees was perfect for football, with nothing around that could be damaged. Admittedly my football wasn't up to much, but sometimes we were joined by the curate, Jeffrey Hollis.

'No sense in praying for Paul if I can't do something practical as well,' he commented cheerfully one day as he stripped off his jumper and dropped it beside me. 'Come on, Paul, see if you can get the ball off me.' He dribbled it towards the house, keeping a wary eye open for the coming tackle. This was real love, and Paul loved him in return, striking up new friendships with so many people who were prepared to put their misgivings aside and pitch in.

At first, I didn't feel he was ready to do too many new things, and we occupied ourselves around the house quite a bit. Paul was quite happy drying up while I washed, so the next week we switched roles. Then, since he was hanging round filling up the kitchen with his large frame, I got him involved in the cooking. He made a macaroni cheese under my instructions, with slices of tomato placed most decoratively on top. One visit I gave him the things to lay the table with, and the next week he had to think out for himself what was needed. He got very proficient at peeling carrots and potatoes, so we moved on to brussel sprouts, then rhubarb. Grating, mashing, sprinkling, opening tins – each new task was planned and approached carefully and supervised anxiously, but as I collapsed exhausted after each visit I was overwhelmed with gratitude to God for these signs of Paul's capacity. So much for the hopeless case who wouldn't benefit from occupational therapy!

Gradually I gained in confidence, and decided, after much prayer, to risk going to the Flipper Swimming Club for the mentally handicapped. We were picked up in a coach to take us to Southampton, so the previous week we had tried a bus trip, which caused no problems. Now my main concern was the water. How would he react after nearly twenty years?

Half an hour later I was laughing my head off with another mother by the side of the pool as Paul, ensconced in a life-jacket, floated past us demonstrating not only his newly-learned arm and leg movements, but his total non-chalance by whistling at the same time. A larger than average ripple cut him off mid-tune, and he spluttered his way back to his feet, looked round and grinned at me before launching off again. He was so stiff that you couldn't say he looked graceful in the water, but it was another new dimension to his life.

Back at home, at the suggestion of the swimming teacher, I tried to make him practise certain movements, and discovered that his left arm just would not straighten, so constricted had he been over the years.

I remembered the isolation 'cell' with its tiny window and locked doors. I thought of the pitiful exercise area with its wire-netting walls, and shuddered at the picture, engraved on my mind, of the man with the strait-jacket: all these things had made their mark, but they seemed now like a bad dream which you remember fleetingly over breakfast.

The cooking went on by leaps and bounds. Remembering that on one occasion Paul had made a victoria sponge, on Mothering Sunday we tried another, which he iced with great care and generosity. From then on he made one every week: jam, lemon curd, and then – Eureka! – perfection, Paul discovered it could be chocolate-flavoured. For the next six weeks he would consider nothing else, and it was as much to save me as to give pleasure to others that we started taking pieces back to the villa for his friends. The staff were quite amazed when I told him that the only part he had needed help with was lighting the gas and taking out the cake when it was hot. His greatest joy came from something with which he certainly needed no help – scraping the bowl afterwards!

As the weather improved we got into the garden a bit, and Paul learned to push our old mower around, with quite a bit of effort. One of his favourite jobs was digging up dandelions from between the flagstones with an old kitchen knife. As I looked at those pathways, laid so determinedly by Alec despite his growing pain, it seemed to me that father and son were co-operating somehow, even though they weren't there at the same time. Paul never missed his father, but I hoped that Alec was somehow sharing with me the triumph of Paul's improvement.

Except for the fact that Alec was no longer there, it would have seemed that the years of Paul's virtual imprisonment had been melted away, and he was now having the youth he should have enjoyed before. Certainly his memory of those times still seemed intact. As we rode to Winchester one day, I told him that we were going to pass the place where Grandma used to live. Half an hour later, with no further prompting from me, he stopped right outside the house and said, 'Grandma.' Later that afternoon we had tea with an elderly great aunt, Aunty Bet, who hadn't seen Paul since he was a child, and they both seemed to remember each other. Paul had taken some buns – chocolate of course – and they had a wonderful time together.

There were surprises, too. I had for some time been visiting a ninety-year-old lady called Emma Street, and one weekend I thought, 'Why not go there with Paul?' I didn't expect them to have anything in common, but to my amazement there was an immediate rapport between them. Not that they said much, but they stared lovingly at one another across the hearth rug, and Emma said several times, 'He's lovely. Please bring him again.' So I did, often. Their relationship was beyond my comprehension, but strangely beautiful.

For me, one of the great joys was to see how reasonable Paul had become, and how able to cope with new situations. Once he came home mid-week and, on the second evening, utterly refused to go upstairs and have a bath. I didn't understand what was going on until he went into the front room, sat down firmly, crossed his arms and said, 'Ambulance come later.'

My fault, I realised. He hadn't been home for two nights together before.

'We must have a little talk, Paul,' I began cautiously. 'Did you think you were going back to sleep at the villa tonight?'

'Yes,' he answered, looking very bewildered.

'If you want to go back to your villa I will phone to get the ambulance to fetch you, but you can sleep at home if you want. I want you to sleep here. I shall be lonely if you don't stay with me. And tomorrow we can do lots more nice things. What do you want to do?'

Suddenly he smiled and said, 'Sleep at home.' That certainly deserved a hug.

Just one weekend started badly and got worse. After hours of piercing whistles and shouting nonsense, which continued in church so that I had to take him out, I felt I had no choice but to phone for the ambulance. He knew, because I reminded him every week, that he could only come home if he was a 'good chap'. This seemed like a crushing defeat, but the next two weekends he was perfect. This was just as well, because I had a special surprise in the pipeline.

The Autistic Society had arranged an outing to Brownsea Island. I was determined that, with God's help,

Paul should have this further experience to enrich his life. There were ten autistics with their families, and a generally excited atmosphere greeted us on the coach, which was stifling hot. We crossed to the island on a launch, had a picnic under a tree, walked a couple of miles, swam in the sea for an hour or so, gathered together again for the crossing, and even stopped at a pub on the way back. So many new experiences and situations for Paul, and he enjoyed them all. I had exhausted myself with the tension of anticipating trouble, but Paul was still a bundle of energy, so helped me to water the garden when we got back. As I watched him filling the watering can, whistling cheerfully, I suddenly remembered the retreat so long ago when God had given me a verse to encourage me.

'Did I not say to you that if you believe you will see the glory of God?'

I knew then that this promise had been fulfilled, and that the rosy glow of the sun setting behind Paul was, for me at least, a pale version of the glory of God I could see in him. From a sort of human vegetable, dirty, static, so bored he had forgotten that any other kind of life existed, he had become someone capable of making friends, exploring, learning and laughing. His private, other-worldly giggle had been replaced by a beaming smile which warmed the heart of any who saw him. The element of fear which had always been there when I was expecting him was replaced by a genuinely joyful anticipation, even though the weekend always left me drained.

Because of this exhaustion, I couldn't quite face having Paul at home for Pips' wedding to Graham – a perfect day for the beautiful wedding service, and a gathering of many relatives from near and far. Pips looked radiant, and I was so happy for her. My brother Denis gave her away, and I thought how good it was of God to give me Paul as a companion before Pips went off to make her own life. She had worked hard to rise above her unusual circumstances, and deserved the happiness I knew was waiting for her with Graham.

By special arrangement Paul came home the following day while there were still friends and relations who had stayed overnight in the area. Many hadn't seen him for a while of course, and they all commented on his happiness and ability to see people as a treat, instead of a threat. I had his hair cut properly for the occasion, and realised how much the shaggy mane and very short-back-and-sides had contributed to the impression of a 'mental case'. He was now a son to be proud of.

Through that summer and into the autumn Paul blossomed and flourished. We cooked, helped each other up hills, had a trip on a canal barge, visited an airport, swam and sang. One favourite occupation was listening to worship songs and adding our own percussion. Soon Paul knew the words and would sing them to himself as he went around the house. I say 'to himself', but in fact you couldn't be anywhere in the house and not be aware of it: sometimes I thought they must be able to hear it on the other side of the road. Although Paul was still not expressive emotionally, I felt that this was true worship of the God who had released him, and that God was delighting in the hoarse voice as much as I was.

One night, for a change, I put on a record of Swedish folk music, and on an impulse decided to teach Paul some folk dance steps. With me leading, and with many giggles, he soon picked these up and from then on half an hour's dancing was incorporated into the evening routine. Although he continued to be very stiff and ungainly in the water, his dance movements were fluid and graceful.

Everything Paul needed for the weekend was kept at home, so he always travelled light in the ambulance, with what he stood up in – and his drugs. They were such a normal part of his life that I had begun to wonder whether anyone was checking that they were still needed. One Saturday, however, he turned up without one of them. I never really understood which drug did what, but when Paul had a very restless night it did occur to me that perhaps it was due to this change. However, Sunday went smoothly until after tea, just before he was to be collected. Suddenly, to my horror, he fell down in an epileptic fit.

I was terrified, because of all the memories of Richard which rushed so painfully into my mind, and because it was so unexpected. I had been told of one twelve years previously, but I had nearly forgotten that. I dropped to my knees beside him, and he came round after a few minutes, obviously quite prepared to carry on as usual. It was I who was still trembling when the ambulance man rang the doorbell, and I was shaken for days afterwards. I prayed that this set-back wouldn't occur again, and indeed it didn't. It had been a timely reminder, however, that only the grace of God through the hospital staff kept Paul on the knife-edge of normality. Most of us can manage without being aware of God's goodness maintaining us, but Paul's improvement was a constant visible sign of God's work against the forces of evil which tried to drag him down. That was how I saw it, anyway.

As the year drew to a close, a new gentleness seemed apparent in Paul. After church one morning, Paul was sitting with his coffee and biscuit when three-year-old Mark toddled up, put a hand on Paul's knee and with the charming directness of babyhood said, 'Can I have your biscuit?'

I glanced at Paul, who seemed more surprised than anything else, and tried to help him out.

'No, Mark,' I said firmly. 'That's Paul's biscuit.'

Mark seemed quite happy with this, and turned away, but Paul suddenly leapt to his feet and followed him. I couldn't hear the quiet exchange as Paul bent down to explain to the little friend at his knee-level, but the biscuit changed hands, and it was difficult to say which of the two was happier.

On the alternate weekends when Paul didn't come

home, I always found someone to take me over to him. He was particularly pleased when it was the turn of John Bartlett, who brought with him his son Andrew, who was deaf, and his tiny daughter Zara. Paul and Andrew would amble along together in companionable silence but with an awareness of each other which showed an unexpected affinity. One afternoon we all stood in a wide circle throwing a rubber quoit to each other, and Paul saw that Zara was being left out, because she couldn't catch it. Next time he had it, he walked over to Zara and put it gently into her hands so she could throw it at her dad.

A lack of awareness of the feelings of other people was supposedly the symptom which distinguishes the autistic person, and even that was being eroded slowly under the hand of God.

By his birthday, on December 15th, Paul had been transferred to a new villa. I wasn't surprised that the staff had seen a remarkable change in Paul, but very glad to have this recognition of the fact. I got over there by bus and train, since it wasn't so easy to find someone free mid-week, and took with me the birthday cake he had made the previous weekend.

What a transformation! Gone were the standard-issue bedcovers, the hard shiny floors and the locked doors. Paul proudly showed me his own room, quite homely with a pretty quilt, a wardrobe and cupboard, chair and carpet tiles. Here at last Paul seemed to be treated as an individual, with some dignity and purpose to his life. Truly my God was a God who answers prayer.

At Christmas Paul was the centre of attention. I felt he deserved this. After all, it was his first Christmas at home since he was seven — twenty-one years ago!

# CHAPTER SEVENTEEN

At the beginning of the New Year a hostel for the mentally handicapped was opened at Knighton, only one-and-a-half miles from home. Knowing that this was imminent, I had spent some time during the autumn praying about whether Paul should be transferred there. After a while I was informed that he was being considered for a place, so I checked that there would be full occupational therapy available, and stressed that this would be very important.

Yet even as the paperwork went ahead, I had no sense that God was saying either yes or no to the move. Still, there was no reason to go against what the authorities were doing. The warden of the new place was very helpful, and suggested that I bring Paul over one afternoon to see the house. We looked all round, and were then offered a cup of tea.

'This is a nice place, isn't it Paul?' I started cautiously.

'Yes, nice tea, too.' He obviously felt that politeness was in order.

'Do you think it would be good to live here?' Paul

sensed there was some purpose in the conversation and opted for a policy of silence.

'It's very near home,' I went on, 'and I could come and see you much more often. Do you think that's a good idea?' Paul looked all around him at the bright new paintwork for a minute or two.

'Yes, Mummy. A good idea.'

In time I had cause to be grateful for his being so near, in more ways than I had thought of. When he actually moved it soon became apparent that the occupational therapy programme had not yet been implemented, however grand their plans may have been. Only five of the new residents were reliable enough to be sent out to the nearby training centre, and the rest had nothing. The warden and house staff did their best to think of ways to occupy them, and I cycled over daily to help, taking the men for walks in the wood and playing board games and ball games. Sometimes this could have been quite a risk – if there had been any trouble when I was alone in the woods with several residents together I would have been fairly helpless. As it was I prayed all the time and there was never anything untoward. Although I knew that what I was doing was second-best in terms of therapy, it did me a lot of good to be involved in this way. One of the wardens said jokingly one day, 'If you carry on like this we'll have to appoint you an official Recreation Officer and give you an office and a secretary!'

When I heard that a trip to the hairdressers quite near to home was planned for some of the men, including Paul, I invited them all in for tea and biscuits, and Paul was delighted to be able to show his home to some of his friends. It all seemed to be going so well.

Then one visit, I sensed trouble brewing in Paul and warned the staff that he might need more medication. This message was obviously not deemed official enough to pass on to the night staff, who phoned me up early next morning.

'I'm afraid we've had a bad night with Paul, Mrs Menniss. We've had to transfer him to the local psychiatric ward.'

'But... but why?'

'Well, he smashed a mirror and attacked the staff who tried to stop him.'

'I'm sorry. Is he all right?

'He's pretty heavily sedated now.'

'No, I meant the nurse. Was he hurt?'

'Oh, I haven't seen her since she went off. Yes, I'm sure she'll be OK.'

'But why wasn't it a male nurse for a job like that?' I felt guilty about this poor lady.

'There were no male staff on last night. In theory there should be of course, but it's not always possible.'

I found out where Paul was, but his new ward couldn't really give me any more information, except that they suggested no visits for the first few days. I felt choked all day, and couldn't eat. The night was worse, until I asked God to show me how to pray. As I lay looking into darkness it seemed to me that I needed to pray against the dark powers of Satan which were working to destroy the progress Paul had made.

After a few days a church friend took me over to see him. The staff said he was no problem, and I could see that in comparison with some of the very disturbed patients here he would indeed have seemed easy to handle. From a distance I could just see a bundle on the floor, curled up like a frightened rabbit, taking no interest in his surroundings at all. I spoke quietly to him, and he hardly seemed to recognise me. True, they had drugged the violence out of him, but all his humanity had gone as well. In one step he had reverted about five years. I couldn't bear to stay long, and in fact there seemed to be no point. At the weekend Pips took me across, but he was no better.

'It's as though there were no personality there,' she

murmured in disbelief.

'Surely he's just in a state of shock,' I suggested. 'Perhaps if he could come home for Easter, and find that home is normal, he would pull round.'

The staff had no objections, so a week later Norma from the church took me to collect him. He still seemed peaceful, but not at all interested or pleased in what was going on. Once home I outlined to him what I had planned. Trying to hold to familiar routines I gave him a cup of tea and then took him to the vicarage garden. To my horror he suddenly walked quickly and purposefully out of the garden towards a busy road, crossing various road junctions without stopping or looking.

I had to run quite fast to catch up with him, and he didn't turn around at all when I tried to ask calmly, 'Where are you going, Paul?'

'Go to that school,' he answered firmly, not faltering in his step at all. I understood from this that he was heading for Oldthorpe and the Special Training Unit there, which he had so much enjoyed. The contrast between the freedom and friendships he had known then and the horror of the new psychiatric ward was awful. He couldn't express this in words, and his features were unexpressive as usual, but I understood how his unhappiness would motivate his escape. Yet on another level he just didn't know what he was doing. How could I help him?

As I almost jogged along beside him, thinking hard, I realised that we would soon pass Norma's house. Wonderfully, her key was in the latch, so I rushed in.

'Paul is making off down the Leigh Road — can you help me?'

Immediately Maurice, her husband, ran out after Paul and tried to persuade him at least to stand still and talk, but in vain. Purposefully Paul crossed another busy road opposite the fire station, again quite heedless of the traffic, and took the slip road which led to the by-pass.

Maurice rushed into the fire station and called the police, while I tailed Paul up the slip road, my heart pounding with exertion and fear.

Reaching the by-pass, Paul just stepped out across the dual carriageway towards the central reservation. Suddenly a thought flashed across my mind.

'Let him go. Let him be killed – then you will have no more worries.'

Just as quickly, I rejected it. 'Oh God, save him!' At that moment, a van missed him by inches, but he was still not deterred, and set off walking about four foot out from the grass of the central reservation. Just quarter of a mile ahead the motorway began. Oh, can't somebody do something?

By now I had crossed onto the central reservation myself, and ran behind him, waving my arms and shouting, 'Paul, Paul, get on to the grass!' One motorist swerved onto the verge to avoid him, and the next, having had more time to react and to see me, slowed down his car to a walking pace behind Paul so that other cars couldn't hit him. Paul stepped onto the grass, and just at that moment, a police motorcyclist arrived. He wrestled Paul to the ground, helped by a couple of motorists, and a police car arrived a minute later.

'What do you want us to do?'

I tried to explain.

'Sounds as though he needs to go back to the hospital,' one of the policemen concluded, and radioed for an ambulance. When it arrived, I was horrified to see Paul being manhandled into a straitjacket. By this time, Maurice had caught up with us, and came with me in the ambulance, siren sounding all the way, with Norma following in the car to bring us both back to their house.

Once back there, I just fell apart. Devastated, I couldn't hear what they said to me, but they managed to give me some sweet tea. They also phoned John Hobbs, who said he would visit me at home as soon as possible, then took me home and waited until John arrived. He came round the door, slipped his hand into mine and said, 'I'm so sorry, Una.'

We sat there in silence for three quarters of an hour. I knew he was praying, even though I couldn't, and gradually my mind felt less numb.

'I must go now, Una,' he said finally, 'to get ready for the service in church.' I looked at him, blankly. 'It's Easter Saturday, Una. There's a service of preparation. Do come.'

'Oh John,' I groaned, 'I just can't.'

'Do come,' he repeated. So I did.

The Old Testament lesson was about the Lord's command to Abraham to sacrifice Isaac. 'He bound his son Isaac and laid him on the altar....' As I heard the words I saw Paul, trussed up in a straitjacket.

The short sermon didn't touch on this passage, but God had already spoken to me clearly from the reading. God delivered Isaac, and Abraham's faith was rewarded. What was needed was complete faith, both for Abraham and now for me. I needed to have this same complete faith, and then God would overcome all this evil and rescue Paul out of his dreadful situation.

On my next two visits to Paul I was allowed to take him out into the grounds, but he scarcely showed any recognition on seeing me, and although he threw and caught a ball, it was so mechanical it was difficult to see that he was getting any pleasure from the exercise.

'I think he's just in a state of deep shock,' I said to Norma on the way home in her car. 'For a month at Knighton he tried so hard and behaved perfectly. Then he had one lapse and was torn away from there and taken to a strange place with strange people. We took such care in preparing him for the last move, but this happened out of the blue. His world has collapsed.'

Norma was very sympathetic, but there was nothing anyone could say. Or do. Except pray. One day as I prayed I remembered that there was a Spirit-filled priest at a parish near the hospital, and I asked him to come and pray with Paul in the hospital chapel.

'Is there anything Paul can sing?' he asked, when we met.

'Oh, yes. "Give me joy in my heart, keep me praising." That's what I want for him.' Paul seemed to approve. So we sang, and then prayed.

To my astonishment, the vicar, Harry Wilson, laid hands on Paul and asked not just for healing, but that he would receive the baptism of the Spirit. It hadn't occurred to me that a handicapped person could possibly have this experience, but as I thought about it, there wasn't any reason why not. Paul seemed very happy afterwards, and much more alert, and I felt that Satan had been dealt a severe blow. Paul's progress towards healing could now be resumed.

Once again, I could praise God from a full heart, but once again, I needed patience. Paul himself was quite happy for the next few weeks when I visited him, but the staff weren't sure that he was stable enough to come home.

I was booked onto a retreat a few weeks later, and asked in advance if we could pray together for Paul. The Rev. Denis Ball was the leader, and he was keen to do this, but first laid hands on me and prayed that I would be healed of the shock of the last few weeks. Suddenly I felt a great peace, and God's assurance, 'All will be well.' Two weeks later, Paul was allowed home again.

That weekend and the following few went so well that I applied for Paul to go on a camp organised by the Mentally Handicapped Society. It only seemed fair to outline the troubles I had had with him in the past, but the organisers assured me that we were most welcome, and that there would be lots of help if needed, so I allowed myself to get excited. It was to be held on a private part of Lord Montagu's Beaulieu Estate, and lots of activities were on the programme. Then, the night before we were due to go I suddenly got cold feet. In a panic I phoned John Hobbs, who came round immediately.

'How could I think it would work, John? He needs routine. Anything could happen. I can't go through with it.'

'But you also know all the reasons why you thought it was a good idea,' said John. 'We need to pray for wisdom and peace.' By the time he left I knew we would go, and that there would be no trouble.

So next day, equipped with our own tent, some borrowed T-shirts and some tablets which I was assured would send Paul to sleep, we were picked up by Phyl Gardiner, wife of the Chairman of the Eastleigh Mentally Handicapped Society. Most of the campers were to be in army tents, but I didn't think Paul would cope with sharing a tent with people he didn't know, so I decided we should sleep in our own.

The first night was quite a testing time. The army had loaned the tents and stoves, but the stoves were too dirty and clogged up to light, and it took all evening to sort them out. By eight o'clock the camp leader decided to go and buy fish and chips, but an order for thirty people took a while to produce, so we had no food until nine o'clock. Meanwhile Paul kept saying he wanted supper. Each time I gave him a slice of bread and margarine and said hopefully, 'Supper later, Paul.' This kept him quite calm.

After this rather unpromising start, the rest of the camp was a delight. Every day was a special treat for Paul, and for me, so great was my joy in the way Paul was accepted, loved and encouraged. He sailed on a large yacht on the river, and had his first ride on a horse, which he loved. He was fascinated by the exhibition of large model railways, and went on an overhead railway. He sat in the sunshine in a pub garden with a pineapple juice, enjoying the friendly atmosphere, and on another day we even went to quite a posh restaurant where everyone behaved perfectly. I had a free day when an army P E Instructor took Paul off to an Activities Centre and returned saying, 'Paul was fantastic: he had a go on everything.'

One day a long walk had been organised, and I felt I didn't have the stamina, so suggested to Paul that we should rest in the tent and walk along the beach together later. When we emerged from the tent we saw Greg, the cook, tackling a huge pile of potatoes on his own.

'Shall we help Greg before we go on our walk, Paul?' I suggested, expecting him to react badly to a sudden change of plan. But he was quite happy, and worked away for three quarters of an hour until he had finished the pile of potatoes we had given him to scrape. When we came back from the walk, there was Greg making packed lunches for the outing next day, so once again Paul helped out, spreading margarine on one hundred and twenty slices of bread while I did the fillings.

Of all the glorious moments on that holiday, this understanding of someone else's position and ability to help out when needed was perhaps the most significant. It represented a great leap forward for Paul. When I thought that the terrible episode on the by-pass had only been four months previously, I could truly say that God had rewarded my faith and that he had wonderfully fulfilled his promise.

As I had so often felt could happen, this step upwards led to another: I reported on Paul's camp activities to the hospital authorities, and said I felt his behaviour had improved significantly. Shortly afterwards, although no one said that my letter had influenced the decision, Paul was transferred from his locked villa to one of the best in the hospital. It was unlocked, the atmosphere relaxed, and it overlooked a meadow where sheep grazed. After a few weeks the Charge Nurse called me into his office. I was surprised to see the Charge Nurse of Paul's previous locked villa there as well, which might have been a bad omen, but both were smiling. Paul's 'new' charge nurse began, 'Mrs Menniss, I've been looking at these files of Paul's, and the reports from his last hospital. I can't think what they did with him. I've never had any kind of trouble like they had there. And you didn't either, did you?' he asked his colleague.

'No,' said the other, 'and I told the administration that I couldn't see why Paul needed to be in my locked villa.'

'Anyway,' the first one added, 'none of my staff have access to these files, so we can put this lot firmly in the past.' So saying, he transferred the incriminating notes to an obscure corner of Paul's file where they could no longer interfere with a treatment of Paul which was positive and forward-looking.

How I praised God for giving me such a clear picture of what God wanted for Paul. The past was past. Without confidence in God that this was possible, without the faith that it would happen, I would have given up so many times. Now we could really start to build.

So many church friends helped me with transport now that I managed to have Paul home every fortnight and to visit him on the intervening weekends. Emotionally, he seemed to go from strength to strength, and if there was any tension I had several friends I could phone who would stop what they were doing to pray. Each time the tension drained out of Paul, and I had another miracle to report to them. I had often thought of both Paul and Richard as a very clear indication that this world is a battleground between God and Satan. Somehow their handicaps stripped away all the pretences and barriers which 'normal' people put up to hide this aspect of their lives. Through Paul, many members of our church were introduced to the immediate reality of prayer.

I, too, was learning more of God's ways. A group from the church went together to Winchester to hear Colin Urquhart speak at a crowded prayer and praise meeting.

His subject was, 'Whatever you ask in my name, it shall be given to you.' By the end of the evening I realised that I had a fairly restricted idea of what level of healing I could expect for Paul. Now I began to expand my vision, and knew I had to pray for God's perfect healing to be manifest in his life.

That year during a holiday on Lundy Island, surrounded by a very special array of birds, flowers and animals, I really unwound and found myself in a new way. All the events of recent years fell into perspective – into God's perspective – and I came home truly refreshed in body, mind and spirit. For the first time in many years I looked to the future not with exhaustion, confusion and fear, but with sheer wonder and anticipation at what God was going to do next.

# CHAPTER EIGHTEEN

To be with Paul, to share in his growing delight with life, was to live a miracle. Always in the back of my mind was the memory of the bad times, and the knowledge that God was now honouring his promise in Joel 2:25 that he would 'restore the years that the locust has eaten'.

Paul was still obviously not a normal person to someone who didn't know him, but to those who did, he was very special. Sometimes he would turn me round to face him and look straight into my eyes — which he had been quite incapable of for the first thirty years of his life — and say quietly, but with emphasis, 'Precious Mummy.'

This happened at unexpected moments, so I didn't always react at the time, but the memory would warm me for days afterwards. To love Paul had always been a God-given duty, part of the maternal instinct, a matter of the will. Now it became easier and easier to do it from the heart.

My feelings may have been changing, but my determination to make the best possible life for him remained the same. If there was any opportunity to stretch him, give him a new experience, or to repeat something he had particularly enjoyed, I grabbed it with both hands. The Mencap Camp, which had been so successful the previous year, was a must when it came round again.

This time he learned several ball games, and although the intricacies of scoring were beyond him, he gradually gained the physical skills needed to keep a rally going in table tennis. He was a real goal-scorer in basket-ball with his long limbs. We fitted in a visit to the zoo, where Paul was fascinated, especially by the giraffes. Even this showed greater ability to relate to the outside world. Not long before, he would simply have been bored. As well as riding, which he continued to enjoy, he had a go at canoeing – strictly in the passenger seat. My courage failed me totally at the thought of going aboard a submarine, but once again Paul came up trumps. A film company was working on a film for use by the National Society for the Mentally Handicapped, and to my joy this included several shots of Paul, riding, canoeing, dinghy sailing and helping out by shelling broad beans.

Everything seemed to be going so well that I was quite surprised after that camp to have a growing conviction that God wanted me to do two things. One was to have Paul anointed for healing again, and the other was to give a testimony in church about him.

He seemed so much part of the church family that this seemed almost unnecessary, but as the weeks went by the idea developed in my mind. What was needed was for Paul to be anointed during a Family Service, not in a private service as we had done before, and I would draw together in a testimony all the threads of what God had done for Paul. I felt this would glorify God, and encourage the faith of the congregation. John Hobbs and his curate Jeffrey Hollis came round to pray with me about the idea, and after a long time of silent prayer, they suggested the very date I had been thinking of. We decided to go ahead.

Some time previous to this I had come across a calendar illustrated by beautiful scenery with a text from Psalm 118. The verse was supposed to refer to the flowers and hills, but I hung it in Paul's room, and in my mind it referred to him: 'This is the Lord's doing: it is marvellous in our eyes.' Now I knew that this was to be my text.

At the service I spoke of God's power being manifested more and more in Paul's life, overcoming the evil of the former years. Then Jeffrey asked Paul to come up to the altar with me and Norma, who represented the congregation. We laid hands on him and prayed, and then John anointed Paul. At that moment the Lord touched me as well. Until then there was still a level at which I thought of Paul as a burden. Now I was set free from that, free to enjoy Paul and other interests in my life. Joy flooded every part of me, healing wounds which I had almost ceased to be aware of, so long had I struggled with them. I certainly knew when they disappeared!

One outworking of this freedom was that I felt able to offer my services in the running of the church. I set off for the vicarage with this in mind, and was astounded to be greeted at the door by John saying, 'Hello, Una. Jeffrey and I were just talking about you. Do you think you could spare some time to help the church?' We laughed together with delight when I told them that was why I had come.

'What we need is someone to visit the housebound,' explained John. 'My health doesn't really allow me to fit this in any more. We can give you a sort of thumbnail sketch of people who need a visit, and I'm sure they will understand if you explain that you have come on behalf of the church.'

Indeed they did, and soon I was setting aside two days a week for this, and feeling really useful as I spent time with people who often saw no one for days. Beyond that I also preached, just the once, taking a day's retreat at a convent to prepare, and having the wonderful certainty that God was telling me what to say.

Soon, the degree of healing I could see in Paul led me to think that I should have him home every weekend instead of one in two. Once again the church, both in transport and in prayer, made this possible.

I was very disappointed in the spring to hear that there were to be no more Mencap camps. I realised that they drained so many resources, but they were incredibly worthwhile, for Paul at least. What it needed was just one person with the stamina and vision to make it happen. I wondered whether I should be taking it on, but not for long. I didn't have the contacts, the mobility.... No, I couldn't.

Yet for many years our holidays had been so important to us as a family, and I had always seen them as part of God's provision to help us through the difficult times. Was there any reason now, just because things were so much happier, that we didn't need a break? I puzzled over this, but I was actually fairly helpless to do anything by myself. It wouldn't have been fair to either of us to go off without other adult support.

Once again it was Norma who drew out of me what was going on, and allowed me to think of other possibilities. We finally agreed that she would take us to the Isle of Wight, where the Autistic Society had a caravan at Shorwell.

Three weeks before we were due to go on holiday, Paul came home with a nasty sore on his lip, which he kept picking at. I told him repeatedly to leave it alone, but again and again his hand strayed to it. The following weekend it seemed quite healed when he arrived, but then to my horror he grabbed a pair of scissors and tried to cut the scab off. He bled profusely and got very agitated. I phoned Jeffrey who rushed round to find Paul sitting on the floor and me trying to mop up the blood with tissues. Jeffrey laid hands on him and prayed, and very quickly the bleeding stopped and Paul went and sat in the garden. Jeffrey prayed with me to calm me down, then left. Paul didn't touch his lip the rest of that weekend.

Next weekend the lip just had a small scab left and Paul seemed to be leaving it alone. But when I woke him on Sunday there was blood on his pillow – he had been pulling at the scab again.

We arrived at church fairly early, and found Jeffrey at the door.

'Look at this, Jeffrey,' I sighed. 'Whatever can we do now? I've prayed so much about this stupid lip, and I feel so defeated.'

'What do you think lies behind it all, Una?'

'Well, it just seems to me that Satan is using this irritating thing to destroy my confidence and deprive Paul of his holiday. But it's such a small thing....'

'But it's jolly effective, isn't it? You're feeling defeated. And do you want Paul to go on this holiday, or are you going to let the devil win?'

I smiled at the way he made me think so clearly.

'OK, but what do we do now? Lay hands on him again? Anoint him again? People will think I'm obsessed with the idea. Anyway there's no time. He's going back tonight and next weekend we leave... if we're going.'

'You're going. You know what to do, really, don't you? I'll see you both in the Lady Chapel after the service.'

As he anointed us both a great peace came down on us, and the battle of the lip was won for God. By next weekend it was quite healed over. How many times did I need the support and encouragement of others to keep fighting? I was so grateful to God that I had such friends in abundance. Within the year Jeffrey had moved on from the parish, but God always provided more friends.

So the holiday was now possible. Norma brought her two daughters Jane and Kay, so her estate car was fully loaded with the five of us and all our luggage. Paul had now enough experience of going away and enjoying himself to be really pleased at everything that happened. It proved to be a truly relaxing time. The girls were very good with Paul and amused him with board games on the floor of the caravan on the one morning it rained. On the whole we kept away from the popular resorts, except for a trip to a boating lake.

Another of Paul's taboos were finally broken on this holiday: we went for long walks taking a circular route. It had become so much a natural part of being with Paul that I had to introduce him carefully to new surroundings, going for short walks 'there and back' until he felt at home in an area. Even on the two camps I had done this. Now on this holiday he took every new scene in his stride. This was further evidence of his healing, for which I thanked God every day. And God had still more in store for the both of us.

A little choral society I belonged to had arranged a trip to Minstead Lodge in the New Forest, where we were to entertain the members of this community and their guests. I had heard of this place, but knew nothing about it, really. After we had sung, we were invited to go into the dining room for refreshments. I was just going down some steps when I clearly heard God saying, 'I want you to come to stay here.' I stopped in my tracks, then realised I was holding up the people behind me. I started to move again, but knew there had been no mistake, so by the time I had collected a cup of tea and turned round, I already knew what I was looking for. There across the room was a tall bearded young man wearing a wooden cross on a cord. He looked at home and I guessed he was a member of the community, so I went over to him.

'How does one come and stay here?' There seemed no point in beating about the bush.

'Come into the office,' he smiled. As I followed him still clutching my cup of tea, God spoke again. 'I am opening a door for Paul.' Once in the office Mike Thomas, as he had introduced himself, gave me a piece of paper which set out the objectives of the community and the categories of those who could stay there for short periods. In this list, printed in letters of gold to my eyes, was the item 'Mentally and physically handicapped people'. I gaped.

'Could I bring my autistic son here to stay?'

'Of course.' How easy it was to knock on a door if you knew that God was on the other side waiting to open it.

Minstead Lodge, the home of the Community, is a mansion set in extensive wooded grounds with a large walled vegetable garden. On our first visit together Paul and I were allocated a small bedroom overlooking distant beechwoods still in their autumn glory.

Guests did not have to pay cash when they stayed, but were expected to work in the house or grounds during the morning to help run the large and rather ramshackle estate. I had visited by myself before we went together, and discovered that Paul was as eligible for this manual labour as anyone else. I wondered how he would cope, but in fact this system was the key to the success of our stay there. Members of the community were assigned guests to help them in their appointed tasks, and it was their appreciation of this help, or sometimes their loving tolerance, which added so much to Paul's happiness. Paul did his best, and knew that this was appreciated. He smiled, sang and whistled his way through the morning's jobs.

One day he worked with Lawrence, loading shrubbery trimmings on to a tractor.

'How did you get on?' I asked Lawrence as he returned a beaming Paul to me.

'Well, I don't know that we achieved all that much work,' he grinned, 'but we had a jolly good sing!'

Indoors, Paul liked helping to lay the tables for meals and afterwards wiping up, quite undaunted by the piles of dishes. When the trolley was loaded with crockery ready to be put away, Paul loved pushing it through to the dining room and putting all the items away on their respective shelves. Once the chores were over we were free to explore the lanes round about, and in the evening we could either join the conversation downstairs or go to our room for our usual folk dancing session. Morning prayers were held every day before breakfast, and I could go to that, leaving Paul listening happily to classical music. It really seemed that the best possible combination of activities for both of us were available at Minstead. And then there were the chickens!

Paul was given a bowl of corn to carry down to the chicken run, and once inside they all bustled around him. I didn't know what he would do, suddenly surrounded like that, but he loved dropping handfuls of corn for them, and bent over to stroke them, laughing with delight at their greed. Then he was shown how to feel carefully in the nesting boxes for eggs. It was a new love in his life, and from then on the sight of chickens filled him with joy. That visit turned out to be the first of many, and feeding the chickens was always on the agenda every time we went.

Paul's conversation was not really up to talking about abstract things. When he talked about Minstead, it was the chickens and the food he mentioned. But I was quite sure in my own mind that what made those times so wonderful for Paul was the love and acceptance he found. Here was a whole community dedicated to believing the best of him. They talked to him, included him, teased him and treated him as one of themselves. There was no talking down to him. He was seen as a valuable human being. Just because he couldn't express that, it didn't mean that he didn't feel it. I was sure he knew he was loved, and he loved in return.

That year Paul's birthday was on a Saturday, and I was able to have a small party for him at home, the first time he had been at home on his birthday since early childhood. He was so happy to see a number of his favourite people, including Elsie Kirby, Joy Wood and Norma. Also there was 'Smiley', the person who had been appointed to visit Paul monthly when Alec died, in accordance with the Mentally Handicapped Trustee Scheme. I felt the effort of working for the premiums was well rewarded by this lovely man, who went way beyond the terms of his contract and was a real friend to Paul. He was actually called Mr Smillie, but with a beaming face like his the nickname was inevitable. For this birthday Smiley collected Paul from the hospital for me and we all had a lovely afternoon together.

Smiley also fetched him for his Christmas stay, which was such a help. We had the usual family gatherings, and now we had a baby in the house, for in May I had become a grandmother: Pips and Graham had a lovely little daughter. Paul obviously didn't know quite what to make of her, but he would look at her curiously, giving an uncertain smile.

In February we returned to Minstead Lodge, because Paul kept asking if we could, and it was as good as the first time. Perhaps it was better because of the anticipation, and in addition to the chickens, which we had to go and see several times, the goats had produced four kids who had to be bottle-fed. Paul just loved helping with this.

In the grounds was a most unusual and beautiful small chapel known as the Sanctum. It was a wooden building with a long wooden sculptured table and another table on which stood a simple wooden cross. The seating was on bales of straw around the edge. I found the simplicity of the room very moving. The love of the community was apparent in the kitchen, but in this place I knew the love of God more directly. At least once a day Paul and I would go there to pray and sing worship songs.

As we sat in the streaming sunlight the shadow of the past was truly banished. Yes, we really had something to thank God for. And we did.

# CHAPTER NINETEEN

One of the clergy who helped in the parish at that time was the Rev. Arthur Collins. One Sunday after church he said to me, 'Hasn't Paul been confirmed?'

'No, he hasn't,' I answered.

'Well, why not?'

'I'm not sure that he would understand the meaning of confirmation.'

'Just because he is handicapped is no reason for not confirming him,' Arthur suggested. 'Every time I give him a blessing instead of the sacrament I know it is wrong.'

I was startled by his words because Jeffrey had said exactly the same thing, and he and Arthur did not know each other. This coincidence seemed to me to be the leading of the Holy Spirit, so I wrote to the bishop explaining the situation and asking whether he thought Paul should be confirmed. I outlined what I thought would be Paul's understanding of the service, and the bishop replied that he would be most happy to confirm Paul.

Since Paul couldn't have got anything out of the regular Confirmation classes, I spent a little while each weekend having special 'Bible story times' with him, and explaining what would happen at the service.

'At the Confirmation there will be an important man called the bishop,' I said, 'and he is going to give you a very special blessing, like the vicar does at the Communion Service, with his hands on your head. You like that, don't you?'

'Yes.' No doubt there.

'Well, this time is extra special, because after this time, when you come up to the front with me in the Communion Service you'll be able to have the bread and wine instead of just another blessing. And that means Jesus will be with you in a very special way.'

At that point, I couldn't think how to take that line of thought any further, so that was the end of the 'Bible story time' for that week.

'It's quite frustrating,' I confided in Norma later. 'How can I begin to put across to Paul all the glorious things that taking Communion means to me? I just feel so close to Jesus, sharing his life, and being part of the people of God, and knowing God within me, but how can I say that? It would be bad enough explaining it to an adult who doesn't understand, but where do I begin with Paul? It all sounds so theological, and you know I'm no philosopher.'

'I suppose you need to start from where he is,' answered Norma thoughtfully. 'What does the name of Jesus mean to him? How does he react when you use it?'

'Well, he often smiles when he hears it. I suppose he connects Jesus with all the times we've prayed together, and that has always made him very peaceful. He knows that we've often prayed for him to get better, and I've told him that it is Jesus that has made him better. He seems to accept that.'

'So "Jesus" means someone he has loved for a long

time, who gives him peace, who has given him a new happiness. That's not a bad start. Does he ever use the word himself?'

'Mostly when he's singing, I suppose. When he's in the garden, pulling up weeds, or cooking, or in the bath....'

'In fact, Jesus is at the very centre of his life. What does he think about church?'

'Well, he's got so many friends there I should think church to him means all the people he most loves coming together to sing to Jesus.' I smiled at the picture Norma had helped me to see.

She spelt out the conclusion we had both reached. 'Who can have a more wonderful testimony than that?'

'Norma, thank you. I've always been afraid of being so ambitious for Paul that I overstepped the mark and made some mistake. I wouldn't want to do that, especially in spiritual matters. Now I can see that being confirmed is absolutely the right thing for him.'

'He's a true son of God, fit to take his place in the church. I'm surprised at you hesitating, really, because everything you have done through the years has been based on that belief. You've been saying to anyone who will listen, "He's not a mental case, he's my son. God made him and God loves him, and God has a future for him." Surely that belief is what has kept you going, even when others couldn't see it.'

'Oh, yes,' I agreed. 'If God hadn't kept that vision in front of me, and given me the strength to go on loving, I would have given up years ago. Only because of Jesus could Paul have found the richness of life he now has. You're right. He's as good a member of the church as anyone else.'

'Better than some. He's taught our church to love. He's taught us a new meaning to love. We owe him so much.'

After this conversation, any doubts were swallowed up in glorious certainty, and I looked forward eagerly to the service.

Then, nine days before the Confirmation, I was coming downstairs when I had a sharp pain in my leg, which gave way under me. I sat down on the stairs, and found that my leg was useless, just as if it was made of jelly. Fortunately my phone is at the bottom of the stairs, and I managed to phone Norma for help. Then I crawled with my good leg to the dining room, into an easy chair, covering myself with the hearthrug as I was shaking and shivering with shock.

Norma came round immediately, wrapped me in the duvet from my bed and got me to the doctor just before his surgery began so he could see me immediately. He examined me, and when he pressed his finger in my groin I nearly shot through the ceiling, the pain was so acute.

'That's it,' he said with a grimace. 'You've torn a ligament in the groin. I'll give you some painkillers, but you must rest – only rest will heal it.'

'Oh, Norma,' I groaned as she helped me into an easy chair back at home. 'I've got to be better for the Confirmation. Whatever can I do?'

'Well, a cup of tea would help, for a start,' said Norma, making for the kitchen. While she was gone, I suddenly found myself smiling. Here I was, doing all I could to bring the healing power of Christ into the lives of others. Why not me? The more I thought about it, the surer I was that all this was a result of Satan's efforts to prevent the blessing which I knew was in store for Paul. 'Oh well,' I sighed to myself, 'if this is a spiritual battle, then let's get out the spiritual armour....'

First I phoned Tony, the vicar of the next parish who was helping out during our interregnum. He said he would come down at eight o'clock and anoint me. Then I phoned everyone I could think of, and asked them to join us in prayer at that time.

From the moment Tony anointed me, I could feel myself getting better. I only took the painkillers the first night, when I slept downstairs. All next day I could look back each hour and realise I was better than an hour before, and very soon I was walking round the house holding on to furniture. On Sunday I was brought Communion after church which strengthened my faith even more, and then Pips took me out in the country. I was supposed to be sitting quietly enjoying the view, when I suddenly thought I could follow Pips, Graham and the baby in the buggy – and did!

Once again, I had many questions. Why was I not healed immediately? If my faith had faltered that first night, would the result have been any different? As often before, I concluded that I was not a person who can give that sort of answer. I only knew what I had seen and experienced. God had again responded to faith, and showed me that he loves us more than we ever understand.

Paul had never been as normal as on the day of his Confirmation. I don't think a stranger would have known that he was handicapped, except that when the Bishop called the candidates to stand in a semi-circle around him, I stood beside Paul. Although I was thinking hard about where we had to go and what we had to do, I still found that I could step back from all that and look at the situation in wonder.

There I stood, a small widow, with what could seem a hard and lonely life to look back on, and a difficult burden for the future, who, to cap it all, had only nine days ago been totally immobilised with pain. And standing beside me was a large rather gangling man, who for years had been dismissed as a tragic misfit to society, shut away so people shouldn't be troubled by his existence. He stood now, proud and tall, making all the responses without prompting. Then he went forward alone, saying clearly as instructed 'I am Paul'.

My eyes filled. That was more than simply necessary information. It was a statement. 'I am what I am. I may be handicapped, but I am a person. I may need lots of help, but I have a name. God loves me as I am, so I love him.' I blinked back my tears to see the bishop giving 'the peace' to each candidate.

'The peace of the Lord be always with you, Paul.' No response was expected, and he moved on, but suddenly turned back as Paul gave his own blessing, loud and clear.

'And God bless *you!*'

Another eighteen months went by. Each weekend at home was filled with walks, swimming, music, folk dancing, games, cookery, and always church on Sunday. Paul was so happy and peaceful at home that I felt all the promise of his Confirmation and the strength given to him by taking Communion was having a wonderful effect.

The fullness of life Paul was now enjoying was nothing more nor less than a daily renewed miracle. Each weekend was like another present from God to both of us. I believed his healing was like a floodtide within him, running deep and strong. I thought I would never take it for granted. Yet it is always easier to remember to pray about a problem that is there than to thank God for a problem that isn't. On one level of my thinking I had come to assume that there could never be any further setbacks.

One Saturday afternoon we were walking about half a mile away from home, when Paul suddenly stopped. I turned round.

'What's the matter, Paul? Don't you want to go for a walk? We were going to see Mrs Street. Come on, she'd love to....' I tailed off, realising that there was no reaction from Paul. He wouldn't move, or speak, but was in the state I had thought of as 'fixed' when he was a child. 'Lord, help us, help Paul, release him from this sickness.' I prayed in tongues for quite a while, grateful that we were on a path behind some houses which no one seemed to want to use. For forty minutes we stood there before I sensed some change in Paul and God seemed to give me the idea of taking out the flask of tea we had with us. Slowly Paul came back to life, his eyes focusing and movement returning.

'Tea,' he said, thoughtfully. I gave him some, almost speechless myself with relief, and trying to take things very calmly and slowly to give him a chance to recover. When he had had a drink we set off slowly for home again, and both needed a rest when we got there. When he woke up again, everything was back to normal, and the rest of the weekend was fine.

The next weekend I had just put his dinner on the plate when he went upstairs to the toilet, and stood there for nearly an hour. At last I persuaded him to come down and eat his dinner cold, which he did very slowly. I had phoned several friends for prayer support, and one of them had come round. When she returned home, Paul went with her, and became 'fixed' again in her garden. She phoned Norma and Maurice, who frog-marched him home. He looked so strange, and I felt very upset. I had told Nigel, our new vicar, about the previous weekend, and remembering his compassion I phoned him again.

'What do you want me to do?'

'Paul must be anointed.'

When Nigel arrived, Paul was in his bedroom, so we had a little service there, and both of us were anointed. I felt God's peace come down upon me, and looking at Paul could see a change come over him. I knew the fixations had left him, and we all praised God together. Nothing spectacular had happened, but once again I had recognised my need before God and brought it to him simply, and in faith. That was all that was needed. Never again did we have any trouble of that sort.

Sometimes I felt that the round of activities that I organised for Paul was just too much for me, and I would tell the villa that I needed to leave Paul there for the weekend. On other occasions, such as when Pips had a second daughter and I spent a couple of weeks helping out there, Paul would have to do without his weekend away. The nurses said there was never any trouble about this, and it was good to know that there was some flexibility. My energy levels weren't always as reliable as in my younger days!

When I could fling myself into supervising Paul, however, the rewards were tremendous. During one of several visits to Minstead Lodge over the next year or so, Paul was given the job of wheeling barrowloads of laurel trimmings through a gate, across the forecourt, across a lawn, along a terrace and down a path to a heap among some trees. I had been instructed about all this, and set about training Paul for the job. The first time I walked along with him pushing the barrow, and showed him how to tip the laurel on to the heap. The second time I went with him until I could see his destination, then watched him unload and return to me. The third time I went as far as the lawn and waited for him to come back. The fourth time he went and returned unaided. We loaded up again, and he disappeared, apparently cheerfully... but didn't come back. On investigating I found him sitting by the heap of laurel – on strike!

'What's the matter, Paul?'

'Too tired.' In my enthusiasm for the progress he was making, I had forgotten the obvious. The community loved this story when I told them that evening.

Minstead Lodge was unique. Through the years many individuals had taken the risk of loving Paul, and at church he was surrounded by love, but only for a short time each week. Only at Minstead could he actually live in a whole environment steeped in God's love and in the understanding that he, Paul, like anyone else, was worthy of trust, acceptance and love. We had gained so many friends in our times there. I became close to Tim Selwood, whose inspiration had got the community off the ground, and who was training part-time for the ministry.

I saw him as the centre of the community, but Paul got on just as well with Mike Thomas, who had first told me about the facilities there, Pauline, who sometimes worked with us in the vegetable garden, Eileen, Cyril and Lawrence, as well as Pearl, who was another regular visitor.

My intuition had told me, all through the dreadful years, that Paul would respond to such love. To have people around me who would take the risk of trying it out, and who would share my joy when it worked, gave me a deep happiness. I couldn't thank God enough.

By the next Christmas, Pips and Graham had moved to the West Country with their two little girls, and this posed a bit of a problem for me. I thought round and round in circles, but got nowhere.

'What are you doing for Christmas, Una?' asked Graham in a typically straightforward manner while I was staying with them.

'I really don't know,' I admitted. 'I want to be with you, but I know I couldn't bring Paul here, and yet I don't want to deprive him of his Christmas.'

'I know you have to consider Paul, but do you think he realises which day is Christmas? If you had him home the next weekend and gave him a party, would he accept that as Christmas?'

This seemed an excellent idea, so I invited several people for the Saturday after Christmas, and confirmed with Smiley that he would visit while I was away. Yet when the day of the party arrived, Paul's reaction was very subdued. I felt awful, quite sure that Paul knew that I had cheated him of his Christmas.

I buried that sense of guilt, but I didn't know how to make sure it was dead first. It simmered gently below the surface, biding its time.

# CHAPTER TWENTY

My trust in God over Paul was constantly being stretched a bit further. One Saturday evening he said he wanted to go out for a walk by himself, and I decided there was no reason to stop him. I remembered that for years he had been trusted to walk round hospital grounds and return by himself, but it was difficult to sit at home, waiting. I prayed, asking God to forgive my lack of trust in him. How could I talk of 'complete healing' if I couldn't let my grown son go for a walk alone? I knew I had to let him go, but forty minutes later when I heard him at the front door, I let out my breath and realised I had been listening for the reassurance of his footsteps even as I prayed.

I could just about cope with that level of independence in Paul when we were at home, and the surroundings were familiar to us both. It happened several times, always on a Saturday evening, and I got used to the idea.

But that summer Joy Wood took us to stay in a caravan for a week, and Paul suddenly made off along the lane towards a busy winding road which had no pavement. I was off after him as soon as I realised he had gone, but someone else found him first. One of the wardens of the nearby Activity Centre had spotted him, and was leading him back towards me. Meekly, Paul returned to the caravan.

Yet as soon as he saw another chance, he was off. Twice more Joy and I had to go looking for him in the car. The last time we had had enough, and agreed that we should offer him a ride in the car, but actually take him back to his villa before things got out of hand.

Paul got into the car, but almost as though he could read our minds, he became very agitated. By the time we arrived back at the villa he was becoming quite hard to handle. The staff, seeing the car draw up unexpectedly, came out to help us. This was the last straw for Paul. He belted away down the path, followed by the two nurses. They soon caught him, frog-marched him into the villa and up to his room, where he was given an injection to calm him. It had all happened so quickly and unexpectedly that it was under control before the disappointment and despair hit me.

'There's nothing more we can do, Joy. We might as well go back.' I opened the passenger door of her car and slumped into the seat, burying my face in my hands. Joy's arm went round my shoulders, but she said nothing for a bit.

'It's not so awful, really, Una. Give him a good night's sleep and he'll probably be able to join us in the caravan again.'

I looked up, grateful for her support, and realised that she only half-believed what she was saying. Yet she knew I needed that hope, and it was just possible she was right. If she could make the effort to look on the bright side, then I owed it to her to try and do the same.

'OK.' I shook my head as if to put the incident behind me. 'Let's have a cuppa.'

But Paul was still disturbed the next day, and the next.

It wasn't until Friday that the staff felt his behaviour was settled enough to come and join us. Admittedly we had a lovely day, with Paul calm and happy. His next weekend at home was uneventful and pleasant as well. But my sense of security had left me.

The following weekend was hot. We walked quite a bit on the Saturday afternoon, through a park and round to Elsie, who gave us a strawberry tea. Her husband offered to take us home, and I felt we had walked enough, so was glad to accept. Once at home Paul wanted to make a salad – the strawberry tea had obviously been no more than a starter to him – and then we had his 'music session', with percussion instruments and folk dancing. Something didn't seem quite right in his mind, however, and he got up in the middle of all this and went out of the front door.

This was more or less in accordance with his pattern of previous walks on Saturday nights, but I was troubled. We had already walked a long way that afternoon, and Paul's mood was disturbed enough for me to worry. Did God want me to trust him as before? I hesitated at the door, reaching out to God in my spirit, trying to sense what sort of battle was going on here. After a few minutes I knew I couldn't leave him.

At that moment a neighbour called Richard came by, and offered to take me in the car to find Paul, if only to follow him from a distance. I was pretty sure he would be making for the river and it didn't take us long to find him. He had already crossed several busy roads quite safely, and he looked quite peaceful and in control of things. I got out of the car and crossed the road.

'Don't you want to come home, Paul?' He didn't look at me.

'Go for a walk.'

Richard was quite happy to continue to keep him in sight, so we watched him until he turned down the path by the river, heading downstream. A little way down there was our favourite picnic spot, and I felt relieved. He would probably sit there for a while and then come back. We waited.

After fifteen minutes I became uneasy again, and went to look for him. Surely he would be coming back towards me, or sitting on the bank somewhere, whistling. But there was no sign of him. Walking faster now, and with a throb of fear which I pushed to the back of my mind, I reached our usual picnic spot, and then ran beyond it. I went as far as I had ever taken him. There was no one. I ran back to Richard.

'He's gone too far now. I thought I'd better come back for help. Where can I phone the police?'

'Do you think you need to?' Richard was puzzled. 'Surely he's just gone a bit further than you have.'

'No, I don't think so. Not by himself. He doesn't go to strange places by himself. We need more help.'

Within half an hour the police had all the details and were out with the tracker dogs. It couldn't take long now.

Nigel came down in response to my call, and went out to see how things were going. I stayed at home by the phone. As darkness fell the tension inside me increased. By eleven o'clock I thought I had prayed myself to a standstill. Then the doorbell rang.

'It's only me, Una,' shouted Nigel through the door as I moved towards it. He didn't want my hopes to be raised.

'What's going on?' I clung to his arm to steady myself.

'They've done their best. They've had twenty police and four dogs out, but it's got too dark now. They'll start again at dawn with reinforcements.'

I could only imagine that Paul had broken a leg and fallen, unable to move, and that they would find him in the morning. I didn't sleep. I prayed, more with groans than words. Hope and fear wrestled in my mind, faith and pain struggled together in my spirit.

Dawn came: Sunday. The morning dragged on. I was brought Communion after church, and told that both the Anglican and Methodist congregations had been asked to provide manpower for a much wider search. Whether the Communion or the news gave me greater strength I don't know, but I believed that such a massive operation would find Paul quickly. Still the day crept on, and there was no more news.

On Monday Pips came to be with me. It was a comfort, but my heart was like lead. That evening an appeal went out on local television, radio and the local evening paper.

On Tuesday Tim Selwood came.

'I had to come, Una,' he said. 'My brother was missing for forty-eight hours in a plane before we heard it had crashed, so I know some of what you are feeling.'

I told him that a large area of country was being criss-crossed by a spotter plane, but that no evidence of any sort had been found. 'There's nothing I can do now except pray,' I concluded.

'Let's do some of that now,' he suggested. We prayed for a long time, soaking ourselves in reminders of God's love and purposes. Praying by myself had become rather panicky and repetitive, but with the support of Tim's faith I relaxed much more. Instead of pictures of Paul lying in pain, or even murdered, I felt the arms of God surrounding the whole situation. The outcome was still very uncertain, but I was so grateful to Tim.

Twenty-four hours later the search was concentrated on the river, with canoes working their way along the banks downstream. Somehow I knew now that I wouldn't see Paul alive again. My grief seemed unbearable.

Yet next morning, when the Police Inspector came with Nigel to tell me that Paul's body had been found in the river, a great weight lifted.

'Do I have to identify him?'

'No, Una,' said Nigel. 'I have already done that, and he looked very peaceful.'

I, too, felt lifted up on a great wave of peace. It was as if God was reassuring me, giving me comfort.

'You have done the work with Paul I gave you to do,' I

seemed to hear. 'Now he is with me, experiencing far greater richness of life than you could ever give him.' I thought of Paul as I had last seen him, walking towards the river, and now God added to that picture a vision of Jesus, walking hand in hand with Paul. I knew, and knew that Paul knew, that he was not alone.

After four-and-a-half days of intense anguish, I was now lifted up to joy and thanksgiving. It didn't make sense, but then this was the peace which passes all understanding, the gift of God.

I knew that Paul's funeral had to be in the form of a Communion of Thanksgiving for his life, and there must be no sadness. The service took place a week later, and a great number of friends were there. Paul's coffin was white — a sign of innocence — and as we entered the church we all sang one of Paul's favourite worship songs, 'Come into his presence singing Alleluia'.

'Paul spoke very few words,' began the curate's address, 'and yet in his life among us, particularly through the great healing of the past few years, he has communicated a great deal to a large number of people. And through him, God has spoken.

'Our world is full of words: words on TV, newspapers, words of attempted explanation, argument, praise, humour, joy, anger, bitterness, words which fail to communicate very much at all. And yet if we could only believe it, we would understand that God can speak to us and heal us in the silence too, in apparent lack of communication.

'For those of us who have known and loved Paul, I am sure we would agree that our lives have been enriched. I think, for example, of that smile so full of joy that would break unexpectedly across his face — a smile of confidence, revealing perhaps a depth of spiritual awareness and certainty of faith that few, if any of us, are ever blessed with. I think too of the enrichment it was to all of us to see the healing that has gone on in Paul. Slow and agonising though it seemed at times, it was nonetheless a very real healing, and this can give us courage and hope in our own pilgrimage of faith. We are encouraged to believe that, in Paul, God has acted among us, and therefore that he can act in other situations as well. And Paul's healing teaches us that God works not only in the moments of triumph and joy, but also suffers with us in our times of frustration and pain.

'In these ways, and many others, we have been enriched by the experiences of Paul and Una. Through these experiences we are surely able to say that God has been glorified, because just a little more of the wonder of God's kingdom has been revealed to us.

'Jesus said, "Whoever does not accept the kingdom of God like a child shall never enter it." How difficult it is to believe that truth, with our desire for more and more sophistication, and our endless chatter and impatient explanation. But I think that Paul, in his childlike way, accepted that kingdom and was much more ready, probably than any of us, to enter it. Now he is there, experiencing the perfect freedom which completes the slow process of healing he showed among us. He didn't enjoy the freedom of expression we enjoy, but surely he now enjoys a greater freedom than we can imagine.'

As we left the church we sang another of Paul's favourite songs, 'Give me joy in my heart, keep me praising', and truly I felt full of joy. Paul was now singing his praises in the very presence of Jesus.

I could think of no place more fitting than the grounds of Minstead Lodge to scatter Paul's ashes, and the community agreed. So after eight days I was taken with several others over to Minstead, and we gathered with members of the community in the Sanctum for another beautiful service.

I had asked Mike Thomas, who had first spoken to me about the possibility of Paul visiting there, to choose a passage from the Bible and say a few words about it. He read from chapter nine of John's Gospel.

'As he went along, Jesus saw a man blind from birth. His disciples asked him, "Rabbi, who sinned, this man or his parents, that he was born blind?"

'"Neither this man nor his parents sinned," said Jesus, "but this happened so that the work of God might be displayed in his life."'

Was it possible, then, that God had allowed Paul to be born autistic so that God's power might be seen at work in him? I thought of all the letters and cards I had received from people expressing how much their faith had been encouraged by knowing Paul, by watching him as he found more and more fulfilment in his life. Certainly, although the idea raised other questions, I had little doubt that in Paul's case this insight made a lot of sense.

Some six weeks after Paul's death, I went on a Christian Family Holiday week led by Gilbert and Connie Kirby. Gilbert had known me from before my marriage, and it was so good to be able to talk to them as I found some perspective on Paul's life.

'Do you feel you could give a short talk about Paul on Wednesday evening?' asked Gilbert. 'If you could just talk about the peace God gave you, I know the group here would benefit so much.'

I agreed to do this, and as I prepared my thoughts, I was very struck by John 14 verse 3 where Jesus says, 'I will come back and take you to myself.' I had always understood this in the context of the second coming of Jesus. This time I had the Good News translation, and I saw that it could equally be saying that Jesus comes to us at the time of our death, and he himself takes us over the threshold of death and into heaven. This meant that my picture of Paul walking hand in hand with Jesus on that last evening was in accordance with Scripture. What a wonderful reassurance that was!

As I spoke at the evening meeting, I could sense the sympathy of this group of people with whom I had now spent several days. My emotional wounds were still too raw for me to cope with too much sympathy, so I concentrated on what I knew to be true, on what I had written out in the silence of the previous night, rather than on what I was feeling.

'Don't be sad,' I told them. 'I miss Paul terribly, but he is with Jesus now, and healed. I wouldn't bring him back to the limitations he knew when he was here. I really believe Paul had fulfilled the purpose of his life, which was to glorify God through his healing. My husband, Alec, was healed of his spiritual blindness at the same time as his physical health deteriorated. He died, but he died a whole person, as Christ wanted him to be. Perhaps there was no other way to bring about his spiritual healing. Paul died, but perhaps he had reached the fullest measure of healing he could in this life.'

Several people had tears in their eyes by now, and it was quite a struggle for me to continue, but I was all the more determined that they should understand.

'When I prayed for complete healing for Paul, of course I didn't think that would involve his death, but I believe now that he finally has the healing I prayed for. Who are we to say that it isn't fair that he died?

'Death isn't a defeat for those who trust in Christ. It's hard for us who are left behind, but we need to pray for understanding of God's timing, and above all pray for greater trust in God whatever happens.'

I believed what I was saying, but that trust and understanding still needed to grow before my feelings fell in line with my belief. Back at home once more, I still had several painful adjustments to make. Tim Selwood phoned me up from Minstead Lodge.

'All of us here very much hope that you won't break off your connection with us because of what happened to Paul.'

'Oh no,' I said. 'I have no intention of doing that. I just haven't thought it all through. Perhaps it would be best if

I could spend some time at Minstead with someone who needed my help as Paul did. I would feel more useful, and it would give me something to focus on.'

'Yes, I'm sure we could arrange that,' agreed Tim, 'but I've another idea. Why don't you stay with my family at Furzey House nearby, and we can go to Minstead from there. If you find it too painful, I can get you back quickly.'

So this was arranged, and turned out to be wonderful. I felt so enveloped in love, just for my own sake rather than out of sympathy about Paul, and it was a time of deep healing. I sat in the Sanctum, where Paul and I had so often worshipped together. The last job we did together at Minstead was to sweep out the Sanctum and arrange fresh flowers on the table: we had sung all the way through. My voice was thick with emotion as I sang those songs again, alone now, but with the same sense of dependence on God. 'Give me joy in my heart, keep me praising....'

That weekend provided a key into the future as well. Tim told me that his family house at Furzey was to become a house of prayer, where people could take retreats and be refreshed and renewed. To be included in this project right from the start, to be able to pray for guidance as the changes went ahead, was exactly the sort of involvement that suited me.

Two more hurdles had to be crossed in my acceptance of Paul's death. First, during the following spring I felt I had to go to the river where Paul was found. Although I felt compelled to do it, the thought of actually facing it disturbed me more and more. I asked Tim to pray for me, and he suggested that he should come with me. I agreed, thankfully.

It was the Wednesday of Holy Week. We walked together to the picnic spot, which held happy memories, and I felt quite peaceful. Then we went in the other direction, and I began to feel increasingly disturbed.

'I feel quite sure that Paul went for a swim,' I explained to Tim. 'He loved swimming, and there had been trouble at the swimming club for the mentally handicapped, so we hadn't been for some time. He had mentioned swimming quite a lot. And then there was that man at the inquest....'

'I didn't know you went,' queried Tim.

'I didn't. Nigel told me. Anyway, it seems there was an elderly man walking along the river that night. He saw a young man swimming, and heard him laughing. He didn't hear that anyone was missing until a long time afterwards, so didn't report it, but they were quite sure it was Paul.... That was about here somewhere.'

'It's certainly very deep just here.'

'Well, the Inspector said that he must have drowned in at least twelve feet of water. In shallow water, a body floats, but in deep water it sinks and only floats to the surface after about four days. Then it was carried downstream to that bridge, where it was found.' I sighed, then made myself say it. 'Where *he* was found.'

'Sit down, Una,' suggested Tim. Indeed I was leaning rather heavily against him, and I collapsed rather than sat. It was a clear spring day, but I could feel only darkness and heaviness.

Tim held my hand and prayed. He prayed for a healing of my memories until the imagined pictures of Paul's body faded. He prayed for a revelation of God's love until I again saw Paul on that final walk with Jesus. He prayed for peace in my heart until the darkness lifted, and I could hear the birdsong again, and feel the sunshine on my face. As a bodily ache can be massaged away, so the ache in my heart was soothed, and I knew I would be able to come back here without pain.

The anniversary of Paul's death could have been hard, but it was also the day on which Tim was ordained priest. As I sat in the service, I was grateful to God for all the friends he had given me through the years. It was as if

Tim, and Nigel, and John, in fact all the vicars and
curates I had known, and all the friends who had driven
me back and forth, given me cups of tea and prayed with
me, were all rolled into one great present from God.

I was thankful, too, that on this day, as Tim started life
as a new priest, I should be made to think of beginnings,
rather than endings. There was a future for me. I still had
an active and useful part of my life ahead of me. God's
plan for my life didn't end with Paul. I had known God's
love before Paul. I had learnt to trust God so much more
through Paul, and had seen so many prayers answered,
but now I could apply that deeper understanding of
God's love in other situations, and go on exploring it by
myself.

Just one more area of pain needed healing.

Christmas was approaching, and memories of Christ-
mases past somehow brought to the surface a sense of
guilt. Paul's last Christmas had been spent away from
home because I had been to Pips', and we had celebrated
with Paul later in the week. This seemed small, but it represented a residual sense of failure. There is never any
limit to the effort one can put into a relationship, but with
a handicapped person this is doubly true. And then, was
my insistence on Paul's independence wrong? Had I
underestimated his needs and so let him go to his death?

Again, it was Tim who drew this out of me, and I broke
down as I spoke.

'You feel guilty, Una,' he said as I dried my tears. 'I
think when you let Paul go out for a walk you were trusting him with the same trust that had brought about his
healing. You insisted that he had a right to his own
decision. Your love for him was greater than the sort of
love which won't let someone go. Yours was a love which
took risks, and that's the best sort.' Tim paused while I
thought about this, but I had nothing to say, so he continued.

'I don't think you are guilty in the sight of God, but you

190

feel you are. Would it help if you made a simple confession to God, so I can assure you of his forgiveness?'

This I did, and Tim pronounced the church's words of absolution. Immediately my peace returned.

That afternoon, I had a rest on my bed. Once again I was aware of God's love supporting me like the mattress I lay on: underneath me, as they always had been, were God's everlasting arms. Into my relaxed mind God suddenly gave an overwhelming awareness of Paul beside my bed, a Paul perfectly healed. He stood gazing down at me as I lay there, with the loving smile that told of his healing and happiness.

'Don't cry, Mummy. It's all right.'

But I did, with joy, because it was.

# Schizophrenia: Voices In The Dark

## by Mary Moate & Dr David Enoch

Schizophrenia is everyone's concern. It affects 1 in 100 people in their lifetime. Every year there are 6,000 new cases in Britain alone. This disease does not discriminate between sexes, cultures, societies, faiths or professions.

This book is for those who care for the mentally ill in families, churches and a wider community.

Mrs Mary Moate is the mother of Philip, a schizophrenic child whose story is so movingly told here. A member of the Salvation Army, she is a voluntary community worker.

Dr David Enoch is a leading Consultant Psychiatrist and Special Advisor to Mersey Regional Health Authority. He is author of *Healing the Hurt Mind*.

Revd Dr Nigel M de S Cameron, Care Series Editor, is Theological Research Consultant to CARE, Warden of Rutherford House in Edinburgh, and Editor of *Ethics and Medicine*. He travels internationally to speak on theology and ethics.

This is part of a series of books published in association with CARE Trust, addressing the issues that call for political action and compassionate involvement and care.

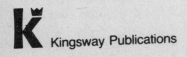

Kingsway Publications